Raising More Money With Newsletters Than You Ever Thought Possible

by Tom Ahern • Emerson & Church, Publishers • $24.95

Today, countless organizations are raising more money with their newsletter than with traditional mail appeals. In *Raising More Money With Newsletters Than You Ever Thought Possible,* Tom Ahern shows why.

"Almost every donor newsletter I see suffers from at least one of seven fatal flaws," he says early in the book. Eliminate these flaws and your returns will soar.

Attracting the Attention Your Cause Deserves

by Joseph Barbato • Emerson & Church, Publishers • $24.95

Think of *Attracting the Attention Your Cause Deserves* as a "Trade Secrets Revealed" book, one allowing you to accomplish three key objectives for your cause: greater visibility, a broader constituency, and more money raised.

With more than a million nonprofit organizations in existence, there's a lot of noise out there. Shouting won't get you noticed – everybody's doing that. And everybody's tuning it out.

What *will* attract attention is following Joseph Barbato's field-tested advice. Take his insider wisdom to heart. It spills over every single page of this groundbreaking book.

Raising $1,000 Gifts by Mail

by Mal Warwick • Emerson & Church, Publishers • $24.95

Whoever heard of raising $1,000 gifts (not to mention $3,000, $4,000, and $5,000 gifts) by mail? That's the realm of personal solicitation, right? Not exclusively says Mal Warwick in his book, *Raising $1,000 Gifts by Mail.*

With carefully selected examples and illustrations, Warwick shows you how to succeed with high-dollar mail, walking you step by step through the process of identifying your prospects, crafting the right letter, the right brochure, the right response device, and the right envelope.

The Mercifully Brief, Real World Guide to...

Raising Thousands
(if Not Tens of Thousands)
of Dollars with Email

Emerson & Church
Real World Guides

First printed May 2006

10 9 8 7 6 5 4 3 2 1

Printed in the United States of America

This text is printed on acid-free paper.

Emerson & Church, Publishers
P.O. Box 338, Medfield, MA 02052
Tel. 508-359-0019
Fax 508-359-2703
www.emersonandchurch.com

Library of Congress Cataloging-in-Publication Data

Stanionis, Madeline.
 The mercifully brief, real world guide to raising thousands (if not tens of thousands of dollars with email / by Madeline Stanionis
    p. cm.
 Includes index.
  ISBN 1-889102-05-9 (pbk. : alk. paper)
 1. Nonprofit organizations--Finance. 2. Nonprofit organizations--Management. 3. Electronic mail messages. I. Title.
  HG4027.65.S73 2006
  658.15'224--dc22
                        2005033706

The Mercifully Brief,
Real World Guide to...

Raising Thousands (if Not Tens of Thousands) of Dollars with Email

MADELINE STANIONIS

Emerson
& Church
PUBLISHERS

CONTENTS

1

Everybody's Doing It

@

One recent Monday a colleague poked her head into my office. "I'm already in touch with HSUS (the Humane Society of the United States)," she said. "No one's sure how bad it'll be ... but just in case."

Ready ... well, yes, we were ready to send an email out for our client. But ready for what happened in the days and weeks that followed? No, not at all.

By the end of that Monday in August – the 29th to be exact – it was clear Hurricane Katrina was the worst natural disaster in U.S. history.

Also by the end of that day, the Humane Society had generated more than $1 million online – much of it from *one* email. By the end of the week, when the depth of the tragedy became clear, the Society had raised $10 million online to support animal rescue efforts, provide veterinary care, and begin rebuilding shelters.

Just as it had after 9/11 and the Indonesian tsunami, the online fundraising world turned another corner with Hurricane Katrina. The tragedy unfolded before our eyes on television, in newspapers – and online – like never before.

Not only did we get our news, volunteer, and commiserate with one another via the Internet, but a large percentage of us took out our credit cards and clicked the "Donate" button.

If you hadn't been thinking about raising money online prior to Katrina, well, you certainly were now.

•••

But apart from crises, there are other reasons why you should be using email to raise money. Let me give you three.

1. Email is cheap
2. Email is easy
3. Email is everywhere

Ah but of course I must add a qualification or two.

■ Email is cheap ... but it sure is easy to make expensive mistakes.

Not long ago, a national advocacy group, chock-full of intelligent professionals, launched an email communications program. I won't tell you their name, but you'd recognize the organization as a reputable leader in the field.

This group jumped on the bandwagon early, building an informative web site and gathering all the email addresses from their rolodexes. Then, to send their emails, the agency signed with what's called a "messaging vendor."

Well, actually, the agency unwittingly contracted with two vendors (they were so inexpensive – just a hundred or so bucks a month). The development department inked one deal, the folks in advocacy another.

I won't even mention the agency's PR team, which for years had been emailing press releases and event announcements through their own desktop email program.

So now we're talking about *three* different inter-agency systems for sending email.

You know where this is headed.

On the day of a legislative setback for the organization's key issue, their disorganized, piecemeal approach unraveled. The PR office sent a press release first: a statement from the organization's executive director announcing their plan to fight the decision and to expect a fuller statement the following week.

Next came an alert from the advocacy department. This too announced the group's plan to fight the decision. But this email ended by asking recipients to contact their legislators.

And then a third email appeared in my box. Another announcement about the group's plan to fight the decision – yes, the same message a third time. But unlike the others, this one included a plea for funds.

Receiving three emails from the same organization on the same day, asking me to take different actions – does that tell you the organization is disorganized and unprofessional? That's the impression I got. And I'm less likely now to take them seriously, get involved, and give to their cause. And, I suspect the rest of their email list is thinking the same thing!

Of course, you can't blame email for this. The group clearly had some communication problems, which led to duplicate messages, confused constituents, and money left on the table. But my point is, the low entry fee to email makes it easy *not* to take the medium as seriously as you should.

■ Email is easy ... or it sure looks that way.

But let's say you've thought out your plan better than this group. You've got your systems in place. You know how to talk with your donors. You've worked out the kinks in your organization's communications delivery. You're ready to go.

Go where? Talk about being all dressed up with nowhere to go!

If you're typical of many organizations, the size and quality of your email list is your biggest limitation. And that's exactly why email just isn't easy.

As of this writing, you really can't buy or rent email lists. Or rather, you can't rent or buy *good* email lists. There are a few brokers and web portals I'd recommend, but for the most part, the online list business is in its infancy.

For instance, only a handful of organizations are buying lists and using them for prospecting, and even fewer are renting or trading their house email list. So, acquiring legitimate prospects is anything BUT easy. And as you know, your program is all about your list.

But even with a list, it's still a challenge. The opportunities to make costly mistakes are plenty. And further compounding the problem is the ease with which a relative newcomer can manage the process. That's great, except that handing the reins to a neophyte can sabotage your program in a hurry.

The result? Errors such as the following:

- Little consideration of how to segment an email list (asking a $100 donor for $50, for example)

- Layout that looks like gobbledy-gook in your donors' email programs

- Links that don't work

And those are only three of many possible mistakes.

It *is* great that email fundraising is getting easier and better every day. But fast and easy shouldn't (and can't) negate solid strategy and good checks and balances.

■ Email is everywhere ... and that's a problem.

Sure, email is everywhere. Everyone's using it. Even my 80-year old dad is forwarding me nun jokes. It is *the* medium. Which is why getting your message to stand out is a tall order.

A few years ago, I worked with a client who insisted on sending an email to her constituents every single week ... on the exact same day and time. Noon, Fridays. Oh, and the same subject line for every email: "Urgent! Act Now!"

Since her response rates were declining, I asked her as politely as I could,

"Don't you think people might wonder why urgent actions occur like clockwork every Friday? I mean, doesn't anything ever happen on a Tuesday?"

She looked perplexed, but I continued. "And have you considered changing the subject line sometimes? Instead of saying, "Urgent! Act Now!" maybe you could say, "Good news you need to hear."

Dumbfounded, she looked at me and said, "You mean I have to be clever *every* week?" Well, yes. There's a lot of noise out there. You gotta be loud to be heard.

•••

Still, don't let these challenges scare you! Yes, I'm aware of your limited budget. And, darn it, I know you probably can't hire somebody like me as a consultant. But even with the resources you have, you can succeed. As this book will show, it simply means you have to work a little bit harder at being smart, timely, and creative.

2

It's All About the List

Let's start with some rudimentary math. If you want your email to generate 10 donations, then:

- (At least) 1,000 people need to receive your message.
- (At least) 250 people need to read (that is, "open") your message.
- (At least) 50 people need to click on the link to your donation page.

It's a numbers game, of course, just like other direct marketing media. It's always about the list. Who they are, how they got there, what they want, and how deeply they're connected to your cause.

Take those 1,000 people. If yours is like many organizations, only about 200 are also on your direct mail file. The rest ... well, how *did* they get there?

Building an online list is the tricky part of raising money with email. And building a strong, engaged, generous list? That's even trickier.

And there are only a few ways to do it:

- Bring your offline donors online
- Conduct issue or advocacy-based campaigns
- Engage in fun stuff, such as flash movies, quizzes, e-cards, surveys, giveaways, and contests
- Purchase names
- Chaperone another organization's list and have them do the same for you

Let's briefly discuss each one.

■ Method No. 1 – Bring your offline donors online

Inevitably, clients that hire my firm are interested in having us build a list of *new* prospects. How is it good for their overall fundraising program, they ask, if we're merely moving donors from Column A to Column B, from their direct mail program to their online program?

Here are the reasons it makes sense:

A) An online program is a service, offering your donors another way to communicate with you. Chances are, they're purchasing airline tickets and books online already. Some will expect the same convenience when making donations.

B) Increased communication builds a deeper relationship. A donor who receives a newsy, inspiring email a few days before your direct mail piece arrives just might be more inclined to make a gift.

C) Donors with whom you have a relationship are some of the best people to help you build your online list. You've already sold them on your cause, and they're often quite willing to tell a friend or two about your good work.

Note: I'm not suggesting you remove donors from your direct mail and telemarketing programs once you've brought them online. Not at all! You don't want to risk losing your more predictable income while exploring this new medium. I'm simply saying there are real advantages to bringing them online.

Now, in terms of obtaining email addresses from your offline donors, there are five principal ways to do this:

A) In your letters, send your donor online to make her gift. Here's an example from the American Society for the Prevention of Cruelty to Animals.

As you can see from the example below, the donor who prefers the ease of making a gift online is given a specific web address (not the organization's home page) to visit so the gift can be tracked.

ASPCA® — MEMBERSHIP RENEWAL NOTICE

The American Society for the
Prevention of Cruelty to Animals
424 East 92nd Street
New York, NY 10128
www.aspca.org

YES, I am proud to be a member of the ASPCA. Enclosed is my membership renewal contribution of

☐ $30   ☐ $25   ☐ $20   Other $_____

To make your gift go to work faster, log onto www.ASPCA.org/RENEW

Madeline Stanionis
Donordigital
182 2nd Street Suite 400
San Francisco, CA 94105-3801

Please return this form and your contribution today in the envelope provided. Please make your check payable to the ASPCA. Your contribution is tax-deductible as provided by law.

See reverse to charge your contribution and for important information.

Copyright © 2005 The American Society for the Prevention of Cruelty to Animals (ASPCA).
Reprinted with the permission of the ASPCA. All Rights Reserved.

B) Ask for an email address on all your printed forms. And give your donors a good reason to provide their address: "Email is the most cost-effective way for us to keep you informed on how we're putting your support to work."

C) Put an insert into your thank-you letters and acknowledgments encouraging your donors to take advantage of the many features on your website.

D) Bring your donors online to buy tickets or to participate in special giveaways or offers. I've seen groups offer calendars, fleece vests, gift certificates, even chances to win vacation trips.

E) Send your direct mail list to a firm that will search databases to try to match your donors' email addresses. This is called "appending." It's fairly inexpensive (15 to 25 cents per email) and may be worth a test. However, keep in mind that the matched names may not perform well and there are privacy and permission problems to think about.

■ Method No. 2 – Conduct an issue or advocacy-based campaign

You've likely seen online advocacy campaigns inviting you to "Tell your legislator that..." or "Sign this petition for...." People who add their names to your list in the context of supporting a particular issue are often excellent prospects.

To illustrate how this type of campaign works, let's take a look at The Humane Society of the United States. Great group, marvelous brand. They use clear, goal-oriented advocacy campaigns to achieve their objectives and to build their list. A perfect example: the Petition for Poultry, a campaign launched in 2004 to include poultry in our country's humane slaughter laws.

On the next page is the email the Humane Society sent to its house list to kickoff the campaign, with key elements highlighted:

As you can see, the organization set a goal of 25,000 signatures. The results? A total of 75,000 signatures – and e-mail addresses – in three weeks, about half of them new to the organization!

That's a resounding success, by any measure.

But, alas, what if yours isn't an advocacy-based organization with national name recognition? What are you to do? There's no denying you'll have a harder time, but it's still possible to use this approach.

You might borrow this tactic used by a think tank. To build their

A catchy name and an urgent goal

Graphic inset contains a quick description of the issue, goal, and how the reader can help

THE HUMANE SOCIETY
OF THE UNITED STATES

PETITION FOR POULTRY
Help us get 25,000 signatures by Thanksgiving!

Dear madeline,

Strange, but true: Poultry - turkeys, chickens, ducks, and geese - are NOT protected by humane slaughter laws in this country - even though they make up the overwhelming majority of animals killed for food in the United States (9 billion a year). Today, you and I have the power to change that.

Some background: Since the 1950s, federal law has required that animals be rendered "insensible to pain" before slaughter. Seems like such a modest requirement reflecting our society's belief that animals should not suffer unnecessarily, right? Yet this most basic requirement does not extend to more than 95 percent of the animals slaughtered in this country *simply because it excludes poultry.*

We need your help to change this shocking situation. To get Congress to amend the law to provide the same basic protections for poultry that cows, pigs, lambs, and other livestock have, we need to demonstrate widespread support as quickly as possible.

Chickens and Turkeys deserve HUMANE SLAUGHTER too!

— 25,000
— 20,000
— 15,000
— 10,000
— 5,000
— 0

CLICK HERE to sign the Petition for Poultry.

Our goal? At least 25,000 signatures on the Petition for Poultry by Thanksgiving, the day when millions of birds have nothing to be grateful for. It only takes a minute of your time to sign the petition - and then, please, tell a friend.

- Click here to sign the Petition for Poultry and instantly join thousands of compassionate Americans who are urging Congress to amend the Humane Methods of Slaughter Act.
- And then... click here to pass the petition on to a friend.

It's that simple to make a difference for billions of animals today - including the 46 million turkeys consumed at Thanksgiving alone. I hope you'll agree that it's time to fix this gaping hole in our animal welfare laws. Please, help us achieve this long-overdue reform today.

Sincerely,

Wayne Pacelle

Wayne Pacelle
President & CEO
The Humane Society of the United States

"HOW CAN WE CALL OURSELVES A HUMANE SOCIETY WHEN 95% OF THE ANIMALS KILLED FOR FOOD ARE NOT REQUIRED TO BE HUMANELY SLAUGHTERED?"

SUBJECT LINE: Sign the petition to STOP the suffering

Specific request that the recipient pass along the petition to a friend

list, the group created a petition on campaign finance reform (a subject of one of their forthcoming reports).

The petition, which was posted on the organization's website, contained only a few sentences. Very simply it said: "I support campaign finance reform" and why.

The think tank first sent the petition via email to their board and staff, and then to their small list of donors and friends. Recipients were asked to add their names to an online petition, to be displayed during the press launch of the campaign finance report.

More importantly, recipients were urged to forward the petition to friends – thereby garnering new names for the organization's list. The petition was never sent to a legislator or used for a political purpose, yet it generated a strong response.

This method can be adapted for your type of organization. For example, a museum might use a petition to support bringing a particular exhibit to town. A university could gather names of people who support the school's diversity goals.

■ Method No. 3 – Engage in fun stuff, such as flash movies, quizzes, e-cards, surveys, giveaways, and contests

Perhaps you've seen the animated online movie "The Meatrix". Or you've sent a last-minute e-card on your niece's birthday. Or participated in a poll on CNN.com. These are all examples of fun ways that commercial and nonprofit marketers are collecting names online.

Here's a review of some of the most popular techniques:

• *Quizzes and games.* A friend recently told me about how her preschooler asked what she was doing as she worked on a spreadsheet on the family's computer. With her daughter perched on her lap, playing with the mouse, my friend explained the numbers in front of her. Bored, her daughter finally turned to her mom and said, "But what can I CLICK on?"

I think we've all got a bit of that kid inside. Quizzes and games, and surveys and polls, feed that child well. They require a relatively small investment in technology – usually a free-lance programmer or your in-house web staff can help you create a quiz or locate low-cost software to help.

While quizzes and games can certainly have a "fun" tilt, I've used them successfully for serious issues as well. Below is an example of a quiz created for The Polly Klaas Foundation to support their campaign to stop abductions of children by family members.

Our goal was to use these short questions to educate *and* collect

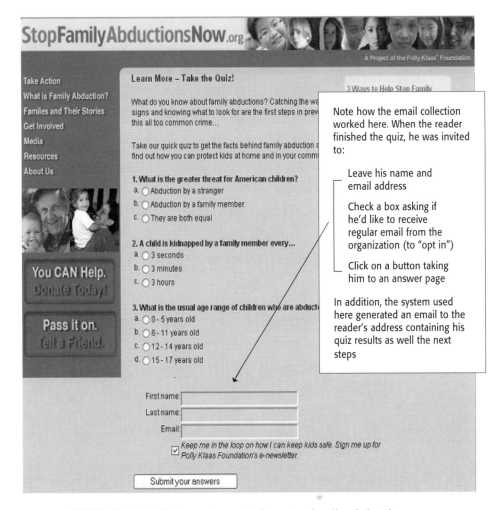

SUBJECT LINE: Kids need your help - stop family abductions now

new email addresses for the organization's list. The results: more than 10,000 new names collected in less than two months. Not bad!

• *Surveys and polls.* Not long ago, an online magazine featured an organization I'm familiar with in its yes-or-no web poll. The question was simple: "Is (Organization) an effective advocate for our issue?"

Take a guess how many people sent an email asking me to vote in this poll? About 20! And no doubt I was only one of many who received their email. People take these polls seriously. And they can't resist them!

The best way to use a list-building poll is to develop a short issue-based question and then invite people who visit your site to respond to it. Once they do, offer them an opt-in to receive news on the issue from your organization.

• *Flash movies* are brief animations created by using "Flash" software from Macromedia. They're used most often to simplify a complex issue or create a humorous or dramatic mini-film and cost anywhere from $2,000 to $50,000.

For list building, asking for an email address at the beginning of the Flash movie, or at the end via a compelling call to action, is the critical component.

• *E-cards.* You know e-cards – online postcards you customize and send to friends. I've never cared for them myself. But others like e-cards and use them. In fact, one major organization says their Mother's Day e-card was the single biggest source of new names for their list.

Typically, organizations create e-cards for various holidays or events such as birthdays and anniversaries. Then, they publicize them on their website and to their e-mail list.

People already engaged in the cause will send the e-card to friends and family. The card directs recipients back to the organization's web site to take action, learn more about the cause, or send an e-card themselves.

In adding e-cards to your list-building strategies, consider a few factors:

A) First, expect to spend between $1,000 and $5,000 to add an e-card system to your web site. You'll need to hire a programmer and designer to make it happen.

B) Remember, the goal of incorporating e-cards on your site is to add names to your list. So when users send an e-card, make sure they are invited to sign up for your email program.

C) Your e-cards should make sense for your organization. If yours is an environmental group, for example, use pictures of nature and areas you preserve for your images, rather than generic images of a birthday cake or wedding bells.

• ***Contests and giveaways.*** A few years ago, one of my clients had an overrun of calendars used in their direct mail program. The group decided to use these to help build the list for their fledgling email program. Within days of adding the offer "Get a free calendar when you sign up for our list" on their home page, more than 15,000 names were collected ... from all over the world.

Turns out, the offer had gotten listed on a "Free Stuff" site. Not only was the organization unprepared to send calendars to Uzbekistan, it was obvious these new people didn't sign up for the right reasons.

That's a cautionary tale, but certainly not a reason to shun contests and giveaways. I've seen many outstanding uses that garner a good response from likelier prospects.

• ***The leveraged gift.*** You don't see this very often, but it can be quite effective. Say you have a donor who intends to make a sizable donation. Leverage that gift by asking her to agree to give you a dollar for every person who joins your email list (up to a certain amount, of course). As the illustration below shows, America's Second Harvest did this for their "Free Lunch 4 Kids" campaign.

SUBJECT LINE: Help feed 3 kids for 1 day with 1 click!

The Quaker company, as you can see, agreed to donate $1 to America's Second Harvest for every participant in the campaign up to 20,000.

■ Method No. 4 – Purchase names

Ah, I wish it were as easy to purchase online names as it is to rent or exchange names for direct mail appeals. It can be done, and I often recommend this approach for groups who have a hard time using the methods described above. But, it's expensive.

Here are your options:

• Working with a co-registration website. This is a website which gathers names and e-mail addresses to sell to organizations and companies.

In essence, the site places information about your organization on its website and attempts to engage visitors via a petition, an e-card, an invitation to sign up for your newsletter, or something similar.

If a visitor participates, she is asked to add her name and email address to your organization's list, and that information is provided to you. Costs range depending on contract size, but hover around $2 per name as of this writing.

• Working with a co-registration "network." Perhaps you've received an offer from an email list broker who will supply you with 10,000 names for a nominal fee. Where do these names come from? Typically from a "network" of low quality web sites that invite visitors to enter contests or receive something for free in exchange for providing their email address. They're cheap, as low as 25 cents per name. But be forewarned: you'll probably get what you pay for.

■ **Method No. 5 – Chaperone another organization's list and have them do the same for you.**

With list chaperoning, one organization sends an email to its list on behalf of another organization. No data exchanges hands. Typically, this is a one-to-one trade: you send to one recipient for every one the reciprocating organization sends to. An example:

A socially responsible corporation that also operates a vast political advocacy program sent an e-mail to 250,000 people on their list inviting recipients to take action with their nonprofit partner, NARAL Pro-Choice America. It was written in the corporation's voice and NARAL Pro-Choice America was promoted as an important cause.

About three weeks later, it was NARAL Pro-Choice America's turn to send an email. They emailed 250,000 people on their list asking them to consider signing up for the corporation's service.

Note that in this example, neither group sent an email simply advertising the other group's offer. Each organization took the time to personalize it, make it relevant to their list, and thus make it feel less commercial. This is critical. Otherwise, your list members will feel as if they've been spammed.

Oh, the results: I can tell you that NARAL Pro-Choice America added about 30,000 members to their list, and very few people complained or unsubscribed as a result of receiving the commercial email.

■ "Tell-a-Friend"

Earlier I alluded to the importance of asking your existing members to help you build your list. Now, I'd like to address this topic specifically.

The phrase "Tell-a-Friend" is quickly becoming overused in email messaging – so much so I'm afraid recipients don't really see it anymore. We've found it's far more effective to give your members specific things to tell their friends.

Here's the difference.

• Example 1 – Tell a Friend

• Example 2 – Please tell a friend about how we're helping Ugandan orphans. Every person who joins in our efforts to find homes and provide desperately-needed medical care makes a difference. It will only take you a moment to change a child's life.

It's equally important to make it easy for friends to tell their friends. To illustrate:

• A client organization launched a petition campaign to half of their list (randomly-selected). About 4,000 people signed the petition. Of these, 15 percent (or 600 signers in total) were new. They had been attracted as a result of existing members telling them about the organization.

• The organization then e-mailed the remaining half of their list. About 3,500 people signed the petition this time, but only three percent (or 100 signers) were new.

What was the difference? In the first campaign, once the visitor had signed the petition, she was automatically whisked to a page allowing her to tell-a-friend.

In the second campaign the visitor, after signing the petition, was automatically taken to a thank you page that contained only a link to the tell-a-friend page. Thus, by making the visitor click to another page instead of combining the thank you message with the tell-a-friend page, the number of visitors who told a friend decreased dramatically.

■ "Viral" campaigns

I have a good friend who's responsible for communicable disease prevention in a nearby county and she laughs whenever I use the term "viral" to refer to marketing. It is certainly one of those buzz words that gets bandied about a lot these days.

Much of what I described in this chapter is "viral" – like a cold it gets spread from person to person. I sign a petition, and then ask my office mate to do the same. She sends it to her brother, and he sends it to his book group. And on and on. It means that what you've done has not only spread to your current list members, it has filtered out and encouraged new people to get involved.

Needless to say, you want your list-building activities to be viral!

■ Banner ads and other advertising techniques

About now, you may be wondering how advertising fits into the list-building efforts I've described here – specifically banner ads and search engines.

Banner ads are the images you find mostly on commercial sites. They tend to be expensive, and seldom if ever are they cost-effective for list-building. I can't recommend them unless you're offered the placement for free.

Search engine marketing is the term for activities allowing people to find you when they type certain words into search engines like Yahoo or Google. There are two types of search engine marketing: paid and "organic."

"Organic" search engine marketing involves tweaking your website to include descriptive, common words people use when searching for you or your services. For example, if you're a homeless shelter in Concord, California, you have used the words "Concord Homeless Shelter" in creating your site. There is more to it than this, of course, and I urge you to begin the discussion with your Webmaster.

The second way to increase your visibility within search engines is to pay for it. Perhaps you've seen the phrase, "sponsored links," on Google and Yahoo. These are the result of paid keyword marketing. It works like this: you choose the "keywords," write the copy, and pay Yahoo or Google only when someone clicks on your link. While the "cost per click" is based on demand for each keyword, generally nonprofits pay 15 or 20 cents per click. It is inexpensive and worthwhile!

■ Tracking sources

One last and important reminder: be sure to "source code" all of the names you gather. Then, for example, if you find your best performing names are those that came in through tell-a-friend messages ... well, you know what to do. More "Tell a friend" drives.

Tracking also allows you to follow-up on an issue or offer for which a group of new names were drawn in.

3

It's All About the Timing

If you take no other lesson from this book, remember this one: to be successful with email fundraising, you must send the *right* message to the *right* person at the *right* time.

Believe me, I know how onerous a task that can be.

Throughout this book we'll talk about crafting the right message. And in the previous chapter we discussed building your email list.

For now, let's turn to the matter of timing and see how email works particularly well when sent at the right time.

■ The internal crisis

You can't be in the nonprofit world for long before some crisis rears its head. A grant is rejected, the water main breaks, your offices are burglarized.

At times like these, putting together a direct mail piece can be difficult and time-consuming. Not so an email. Case in point: When a fire destroyed parts of the Massachusetts SPCA's primary shelter and animal hospital, the organization turned to its supporters within hours. This simple, text email brought in thousands of dollars immediately:

```
--------------------------------
Massachusetts SPSA July 17, 2002
Fire at Boston Shelter and Angell Memorial Animal
Hospital!
--------------------------------

Dear Madeline,

Today, a fire forced the evacuation of almost 400
employees and 130 animals from the Jamaica Plain,
Mass., home of Angell Memorial Animal Hospital, the
MSPCA Boston Animal Shelter, and MSPCA administrative
headquarters.

The good news: All of us - animals and people - are
okay. MSPCA employees and Boston firefighters
demonstrated amazing compassion and courage in
saving the lives of animals. They rapidly formed a
relay line to carry more than 100 animals out of the
smoke-filled building to safety.

Shelter animals have been relocated to MSPCA and other
shelters. In addition, some animals were admitted to
Angell Memorial Animal Hospital for observation and
smoke inhalation. Animals evacuated from Angell have
been returned to the hospital wards, which were not
damaged in the fire.

For more information about the fire, click here:
http://1v0.net/URL.asp?1_monns3780-18673

Donations to support the care of Shelter animals can be
sent to our Pet Care Assistance Fund:
http://1v0.net/URL.asp?2_monns3780-18673

Thank you for your continued compassion and support.

Dr. Gus W. Thornton
President, MSPCA
```

SUBJECT LINE: Fire at Boston Shelter and Angell Memorial Animal Hospital

A number of elements make a crisis email like this one successful.

• First, the crisis must be *real*. Your constituents will grow cynical in a hurry if you invent a dire situation every three months.

• Second, the writing must be heartfelt and honest. Readers will respond if you share not only how the crisis has impacted your work, but your own personal feelings as well.

• The final key to success is immediacy – the topic of this chapter. Your email must have an up-to-the-minute feel. An urgency. "This is going on NOW" is what you want to convey to readers.

■ Natural or man-made disasters

September 11, the tsunami … we're all familiar with the online response to disasters, and with good reason. Upwards of $350 million in relief funds poured in online within weeks of the Asian tsunami. And hundreds of thousands of people donated online for the first time.

Thankfully, catastrophes of this magnitude are rare. But there are other disasters, such as hurricanes, when an organization must reach out immediately.

Such was the case when the Humane Society of the United States responded to the needs of animals during devastating hurricanes in Florida. As each new hurricane hit, the Society sent constituents an email offering an on-the-ground look at the relief teams and asking for help.

The first email, shown on the next page, hit a few days after the first hurricane, when Humane Society disaster teams were able to enter the region. This and subsequent emails were written from the point of view of the disaster team leader, and included photos of the work at hand (an important element).

DISASTER UPDATE

From the pet experts at...

THE HUMANE SOCIETY OF THE UNITED STATES

A Special Report from our Disaster Animal Response Team

Help Us Out!

Donate Now

Dear Animal Lover,

The devastation of Hurricane Charley is all around me. It's Wednesday, and the situation for animals here in southwestern Florida remains dire. We at The Humane Society of the United States (HSUS) are working around the clock to save as many as we can.

At our disaster relief center here in Punta Gorda, one of the hardest hit areas, we first began accepting animals on Monday. This facility is taking in rescued, displaced, and injured animals, and caring for them until they can be transferred to local shelters.

Even as you read this, fresh HSUS Disaster Animal Response Teams (DART) are stepping up operations in nearby counties. Our highly trained teams have been on site since Saturday, conducting damage assessments from the hurricane and coordinating rescues daily with county animal control officers.

Thankfully, we've had some heartwarming

This dog found the safety of HSUS's Disaster Relief Center in Punta Gorda, Florida.

Our Disaster Animal Response Teams have been working nonstop in Florida since Saturday.

Please help The Humane Society of the United States in our crucial disaster response mission with a special donation today.

We'll put your donation to work immediately to help animals hurt by Hurricane Charley and future disasters.

SUBJECT LINE: A special Hurricane Charley report

The next email (shown at right) was sent on the heels of the third hurricane to those who had already given. The copy acknowledges their gift and asks for another. Donors are also strongly encouraged

THE HUMANE SOCIETY OF THE UNITED STATES.

HURRICANE UPDATE: An unprecedented string of natural disasters

Dear Kristin,

Today, I am in Florida responding to yet another hurricane, Ivan. I have many years of experience in responding quickly to disasters, and I can tell you that **I have never experienced such a devastating string of natural disasters**. In fact, it's the worst series in the Humane Society of the United States's 50-year history.

That's why I'm writing to you now. You have already been so generous, but we need more help. You may not know this, but **our relief efforts are funded entirely by donations**. And after spending the last month operating very similar efforts for Hurricanes Charley and Frances, I can tell you that our resources are stretched thin. Here's how you can help:

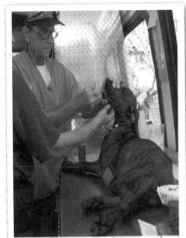

Three hurricanes in a month have stretched our resources - - Please help, if you can.

1. Please let others know how desperately pets and people need help right now. Simply forward this email to your friends and family, or send them this link: **https://secure.hsus.org/01/ivan_e?source=drfha7**

2. If you can, please make another gift to help to save as many pets and other animals as we can. **Click here to pitch in - again - $5 or $500, every little bit helps today**.

SUBJECT LINE: ANOTHER hurricane - more animals need help

to forward the email to their friends.

The final email (shown below) was long. A story, really, about the very real difficulties the disaster team is facing and an invitation to watch a heartwarming video of their work (which 40 percent of those

THE HUMANE SOCIETY
OF THE UNITED STATES

Hurricane Update:
Where are the animals?

Dear Kristin,

First, **thank you**. Your contributions are making it possible for us to help people and pets in Florida face their fourth hurricane in less than two months. If you haven't had a chance to pitch in, there's still time. **Click here.**

To put it simply, **Hurricanes Charley, Frances, Ivan, and now Jeanne have devastated many parts of Florida and the Gulf Coast.** . If you are fortunate enough never to have personally experienced this kind of natural disaster, I'd like to share with you a glimpse of what our Disaster Animal Response Teams have been facing - and show you how your contributions have been put to work. **Click here to watch our brief video** (and I assure you that it's heartwarming, not disturbing).

SEE your contributions at work saving animals. **Click here.**

The HSUS's National Disaster Animal Response Teams are moving into the affected areas of eastern Florida as I write this. While exhausted from the three recent hurricanes, our teams know what to expect now and have already started relief efforts. Like last week (and the weeks before that), we know that our teams will be combing the region, walking door to door in neighborhoods ravaged by debris, sand, and water, looking for animals.

It can be heartbreaking, challenging work. Last week, in the Gulf Coast, our teams encountered sand everywhere - sand that for days prevented rescue workers even from entering the barrier islands. Just in our first few hours of work, we could tell there were animals to save: cat tracks dotted the sand that covered virtually every square foot of one island, and a dog howled in the distance, clearly hungry and alone.

SUBJECT LINE: Hurricane Update: Where are the animals?

receiving this email did).

As for the results, the Humane Society, in good measure because of these emails, generated more than $340,000 from 8,200 donors.

■ The news

Your director receives a MacArthur genius award. A young family you've been serving is moving into a house built by Habitat for Humanity.

At some point, your group – or the issue you address – may be thrust into the news.

Whether it's capitalizing on good news or countering bad press, this is often a prime time to launch an email.

Take the case of NARAL Pro-Choice America, a women's advocacy organization.

Within minutes of the U.S. Senate passing the so-called "partial-birth" abortion legislation a few years ago, NARAL Pro-Choice America sent an email to its constituents.

 NARAL Pro-Choice America

When one right falls, what's next?

Dear Rachel,

Just minutes ago, Congress sent the so-called "partial-birth" abortion ban to the President's desk - Bush has vowed to sign it, which will make him the first president since *Roe v. Wade* to criminalize safe abortion procedures.

Bush's interference in private medical decisions is no surprise. It's just the latest step in his campaign to take away a woman's right to choose. But believe me, Bush and his anti-choice friends have more anti-choice laws waiting in the wings.

Rachel, we can't afford four more years of Bush undermining our privacy and a woman's right to choose at every turn. If he is re-elected, it could mean the end of *Roe* as we know it. It comes down to this: our only recourse is to stop Bush from being re-elected. Please click here to help us right now with a gift to elect a pro-choice president.

Taking away a woman's right to choose is within their grasp...and they know it.

This the first of many moves Congress will take to completely take away our reproductive rights.

We have one year. Only one year to get the message to the millions of Americans who can elect a pro-choice president. It will take the leadership, action, and generosity of every single one of us. Please, I urge you to start right now. Make a gift to help elect a pro-choice president. Contribute to save a woman's right to choose today. Click here.

* Make an emergency contribution, right now.

Then, tell your friends why women can't afford four more years of Bush's anti-choice, anti-privacy policies. Click here to spread the word.

SUBJECT LINE: A dark day for women's rights

The email echoed the feelings of its supporters, summarized the measures the organization would take, and urged members to support the plan.

This single email garnered the highest-ever returns for the organization.

When recipients clicked on "Make an emergency contribution," they were sent to the donation page (shown below) NARAL

 **NARAL** Pro-Choice America   *When one right falls, what's next?*

Your generous gift today will enable NARAL Pro-Choice America to fight the criminalization of safe abortion procedures. Right now, we are set to launch our most important effort in decades: mobilizing pro-choice America in the fight to save a woman's right to choose through television commercials, grassroots organizing, online activism, media outreach and much more.

With your help we will save a woman's right to choose: one person, one city and one state at a time.

Please select a donation amount:

○ $35
○ $50
○ $75
○ $100
○ $1,000
○ Other: $ _____
   Minimum payment: $5

Complete the following to make your gift:

Payment method: *
[Visa ▾]

Card number: *
[_____]

Expiration date: *
[01 ▾] [2005 ▾]

Email: *
[_____]

First Name: *
[_____]

Last Name: *
[_____]

Address Line 2:
[_____]

City: *
[_____]

State *
[--Choose a State-- ▾]

Zip: *
[____] - [____]

* Required field

[Make my gift now!]

We will be happy to send you materials about a wide range of issues relating to a woman's right to choose and how you can help protect choice. Click here.

Donations to NARAL Pro-Choice America are not tax deductible and may be used for supporting or opposing political candidates. NARAL Pro-Choice America does not accept contributions from business corporations or labor organizations. The first $10.00 of your annual renewal donation keeps your membership status active.

You can contact us at membership@naral.org or you can write to us at: NARAL Pro-Choice America, 1156 15th Street, NW, Washington, DC 20005. You can also contact us at (202) 973-3000.

Pro-Choice America had customized for the campaign. Not only did the text and images match the email, the page was preprinted with the donor's name and address.

■ Other types of time-sensitive emails

Thus far, we've talked about crises, news, and natural disasters as suitable times to send email appeals. But, what if your organization isn't a part of any of these events? Can you still take advantage of timing? Certainly ... and it's not that difficult.

Seasons. Say, for example, yours is a group providing homeless services. You might send an e-mail appeal on the day the temperature first drops below freezing, making your services all the more critical. Or maybe you run a summer program for disadvantaged youth. Launch an email on the first day of summer camp.

Somebody else's news. "The Hazards of Obesity." It's a three-part series your local daily is running. While the story isn't directly about your health agency, here's a prime time to send an email discussing the subject and telling your supporters what you're doing about it.

Tie-in with an event. Do you have a gala dinner or other special event every year? Only so many people can attend. Get permission from your eloquent keynote speaker to send her speech as part of an email appeal the following morning.

■ Taking advantage of timing

As we all know, crises aren't (often) predictable, and disasters don't observe a schedule. Still you can take certain steps to prepare yourself to respond quickly to unexpected events. Among the most important are the following:

- *Systems.* Of course you'll need the technology in place. But beyond this you'll also need to know who will do what. For example, who will write copy? Who will approve it? Who will launch your message? You don't want to miss your opportunity because of confusion over responsibility.

• *Emergency donation pages.* The companion to all your email messages, emergency or not, are the donation pages where your recipients make their gifts. You'll be smart to have a donation page already set up and tested. Then you can simply (and quickly) add text and maybe an image about your emergency.

• *A little experience.* It's best if you've already been communicating with your constituents via email. Not only will they have come to see you as a known and trusted source, but you will have also worked out the kinks in your email system.

• *Preparation.* In the case of an *expected* outcome (such as a vote in Congress) prepare and test your message in advance. Take a page from the best obituary writers: have 90 percent of your text prepared in advance. Don't wait until that fateful day to put it all together.

• *The right attitude.* Be ready to think "Web/email" when something critical happens. Your constituents will look to you for the latest news and how they can help. And they'll be looking on the Web first. Be ready!

4

Think Campaigns, Not Appeals

I went out on a lot of dates in high school. More specifically, *first* dates. So many in fact I just don't remember most of them. Sort of reminds me of email.

An email is lot like a first date. Sometimes, the timing is right. The chemistry is there. And you click. At other times, you had a terrible day and were preoccupied – then it's over before it's begun.

An email *campaign* is a little different, more like a *relationship*. It's coffee this week, dinner the next, and a movie on Saturday. Or, an email this week, a mention in your e-newsletter the next, and a last chance email to boot.

In successful email fundraising, a campaign approach in which you send a series of email messages about your offer can make a big difference, for a few reasons.

First, the volume of emails your constituents receive daily is likely to be greater than the number of mail appeals and phone calls they receive. And you know how hard it is to get a respectable response from those media! Quite often an email is simply missed.

Second, email has a limited shelf life. You'll know quickly how your message is performing. The vast majority of responses will arrive within 48 hours. Oh, gifts will trickle in thereafter ... but for the most part, people tend to respond to email immediately or not at all.

Combined, these factors argue for repeated attempts to reach your recipient's in-box.

■ When should you run a campaign?

One could argue you should run an email campaign frequently. That's not a bad idea but it's not always possible. It takes a certain amount of planning and execution so you'll want to choose your campaigns wisely. Here are several elements to consider:

• Campaigns lend themselves to specific and time-sensitive projects or special opportunities, such as a matching gift or sponsoring a new program.

• Campaigns are particularly effective around news or issues that already have your donor's attention.

• Holidays – end of the year, Mother's Day – are perfect, since there's a build-up and a deadline.

Let's take a look at a few examples.

• Campaign No. 1 – Year-end

Most groups already have a year-end fundraising program in place. Email opens up all sorts of new possibilities to enhance this effort.

Earthjustice, a law firm for the environment recently used a simple, three-part series for their year-end campaign.

Shown on the next page is the first email, thanking donors for their support. It was sent to the entire online list during the

Thanksgiving season. The selection of the right photo was the most time-consuming part of this piece. Earthjustice needed something striking and memorable (this black and white version pales in comparison to the original).

SUBJECT LINE: Thank you from Earthjustice

The second email, shown on the next page, raised the issue of year-end giving, as evident from the headline. Sent mid-December, this email generated a modest response, but it also effectively set the stage for the email that followed.

Make Earthjustice a Year-End Giving Priority

Your support can help us prevent irretrievable losses of wildlife and special places in 2005

Click here to make your tax-deductible year-end gift

EARTHJUSTICE
Because the earth needs a good lawyer

Photo by Galen Rowell/Mountain Light

Dear Adelaide,

As 2004 comes to a close, we have arrived at a defining moment for everyone who cares deeply about protecting the earth's beauty and diversity.

You are our partner in that mission and, as the new year begins, it is clear where we must set our sights in the current political climate. We must prevent the irretrievable loss of wildlife and special places that could not be fixed by a subsequent administration or another Congress.

Through strategic case selection, new communications tactics, and invigorated coalition building, Earthjustice has a strong and innovative plan for meeting the challenges we will face from the Bush administration and its allies in industry and Congress. But we need you with us to put that plan into action. **Please help ensure we have the resources we need in 2005 by making a tax-deductible year-end gift**.

The Bush administration's renewed effort to impose a disastrous energy policy, including drilling in the pristine Arctic National Wildlife Refuge and Alaska's Western Arctic, is just one example of the attacks we must counter to protect our public lands, wildlife, air, and water.

As we face the toughest political situation we have ever seen, your active participation and generous financial support are absolutely essential. **Please, make your tax-deductible gift to Earthjustice a personal year-end giving priority.** Your generosity is what will allow us to achieve important victories in 2005.

Thank you in advance for your support, and warmest wishes for a safe and happy holiday season!

Sincerely,

Vawter "Buck" Parker
Executive Director
Earthjustice

SUBJECT LINE: Make Earthjustice a Year-end Giving Priority

Shown on the next page, the third email, again stressing year-end giving, landed in recipients' in-boxes toward the last day of the year (something difficult to achieve with direct mail). The bulk of the campaign revenue came in as a result of this message.

There's still time!

Make your tax-deductible year-end gift to Earthjustice by December 31st

Photo: Tom Darin

Photo: Center for Biological Diversity

Photo: Katerina Zelena

EARTHJUSTICE
Because the earth needs a good lawyer

Dear Adelaide,

As we look forward to 2005, there's no denying this fact: Never in American modern history have Congress and the White House been so hostile to environmental progress.

So why am I writing to ask you to share my spirit of optimism and resolve?

Not just because despair is not an option, but because over the past four years, Earthjustice's ability to hold the line--and force the administration to uphold the law--has been proven time and time again by our accomplishments as the lawyers for the Natural Resources Defense Council, the Sierra Club, The Wilderness Society, and hundreds of other national, regional, and local groups.

In the last year we have:

- Prevented oil and gas leasing in hundreds of thousands of acres of scenic national forest lands south of Yellowstone National Park

- Secured protections for Puget Sound's Southern Resident Orcas to help these magnificent creatures recover from the brink of extinction

- Halted logging in key roadless areas of the Tongass National Forest, the world's largest intact temperate rainforest

As these and our other victories show, we must not despair... we must act. The environment needs your energy, your passion, and your commitment. **Please stand with us and help us prepare for the work ahead in 2005 by making your tax-deductible year-end gift here.**

I promise you this: With your generous year-end help, Earthjustice will seize every opportunit to challenge assaults on our air, water, public lands, and wildlife. We will actively oppose changes in environmental laws that would weaken protections for the natural treasures we cherish.

Please make your tax-deductible gift to Earthjustice a personal year-end giving priority. Your generosity is what will allow us to achieve important victories in 2005.

As we prepare for the year ahead, I am confident that you will be with us. Thank you in advance for your generosity.

Sincerely,

Vawter "Buck" Parker
Executive Director
Earthjustice

SUBJECT LINE: There's still time!

All of the emails linked to a donation page (shown below) that repeated the key points and images of the series and offered donors convenient ways to give beyond simply completing the form online (a nice touch!). Further, the page was preprinted with the donor's name and address, making it a cinch to complete.

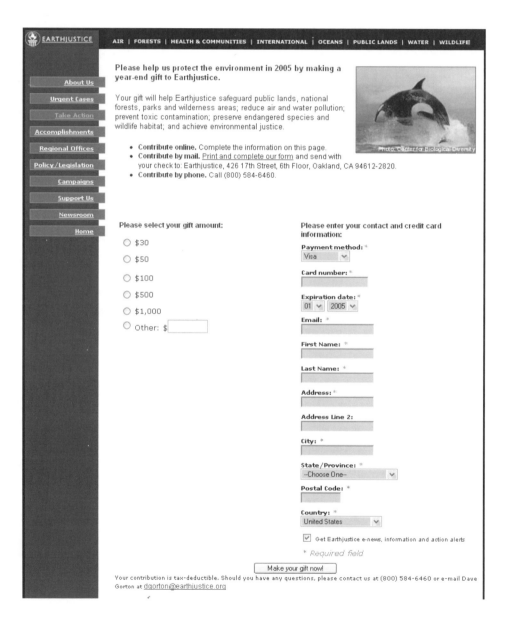

The results

When this campaign was conducted, Earthjustice's email list totaled about 56,000. The table below shows the results: greater than a one-percent response rate and $100,000 in revenue. A satisfactory effort, to be sure.

Total recipients	# Gifts	Response rate	Total donated	Average gift
56,636	599	1.28%	$108,649	$181.38

- **Campaign No. 2: Supporting a specific project**

One of the most common ways to raise money with email is to highlight specific projects. This could be money to buy new playground equipment, send youth leaders to a training conference, or in the case of the Union of Concerned Scientists (UCS) to place an ad in a number of wide-circulation publications.

The issue at hand for UCS was combating what the organization considered a deceptive advertising campaign by a major automakers' group. It's important to note that the issue wasn't particularly newsworthy (had it been, the campaign would have performed even better!).

The campaign series was comprised of four emails.

The first, shown on the next page, was an "action alert" urging UCS members to call for an investigation of the automaker's claim that "Autos manufactured today are virtually emission-free." Readers could click on a link to see the automaker's ad and find out why UCS thought it was misleading.

Automaker Ad Deceives Public & Lawmakers

The Auto Alliance, the lobbyist group representing most major automakers, has launched a deceptive new ad campaign claiming, "Autos manufactured today are virtually emission-free." Not only are today's passenger vehicles emitting more global warming pollution than 20 years ago, but some vehicles made in 2005 will have forty times the smog-forming emissions of a Ford Escape Hybrid or Toyota Prius. Using factual omissions to hide polluting emissions is unacceptable. Please contact the Federal Trade Commission and ask that they immediately open a false advertising investigation on the Alliance.

(TAKE ACTION)

Read the Letter:

Lydia B. Parnes
Acting Director, Bureau of Consumer Protection

The Auto Alliance Ad

ad reprinted from *Congress Daily*

Click here to see the full ad and why it is misleading

Instructions

SUBJECT LINE: Automakers pollute the press

Following the alert, UCS developed an ad about the issue, shown in the next email, and invited recipients to support its placement in several publications. The ad was featured near the top, with the offer described below it. Readers could grasp immediately what UCS was trying to do.

UCS also created momentum by placing the goal (570 supporters at $34 each) underneath the child's picture.

Union of Concerned Scientists
Citizens and Scientists for Environmental Solutions

Expose Auto Alliance Deception

Dear Madeline,

Last week, we told you that the Auto Alliance, the lobbyist group representing most major automakers, is running deceptive ads using a messy toddler in a car seat to humorously attest to new autos' cleanliness "under the hood." The ad then claims:

"Autos manufactured today are virtually emission-free."

This outrageous, blatantly false claim is central to the Auto Alliance's advertising campaign targeting legislators. They are essentially telling our nation's lawmakers that their "job is done" and further emission regulations would be unneeded burdens on an environmentally responsible industry. However, today's cars, trucks, minivans and SUVs are emitting **more** global warming pollution than they did 20 years ago.

It's unbelievable! And even worse, the Auto Alliance's false claims are coming on top of its lawsuit to block landmark regulations to curb global warming emissions from automobiles. We've already asked the Federal Trade Commission (FTC) to investigate the auto industry's claims and enforce "truth-in-advertising" rules. (If you have not already taken action, **click here to support the investigation**.) But with an issue this important, we cannot merely rely on the FTC to do the right thing.

That's why we're also fighting back in another way, and we urgently need your help to make it happen. We're placing ads, starting with the very places Auto Alliance advertised, that expose their deceptive campaign. Will you help us? Simply **click here to make an online contribution** to underwrite placement of the ads.

This is a hard-hitting response but we cannot let the Auto Alliance get away with misrepresentations that are harmful to consumers, the environment, and public health. Your help is critical to maximizing the visibility of our ad. **If 570 supporters donate $35 each, we can do it.**

With your support today, UCS will expose the Auto Alliance's deceptive ad campaign and make sure Congress and consumers know that pollution from new cars, trucks, and SUVs is still a major problem that cannot be ignored or covered up.

> **IF TODAY'S CARS ARE 'VIRTUALLY EMISSION FREE'**
>
> **...THEN SO IS THIS CIGARETTE.**
>
> Help us place our response ad above to expose the Auto Alliance's false claims! If 570 supporters donate $35 each, we can do it. Click here.

Thank you,

Kevin Knobloch
President

P.S. To learn more about the auto industry's false ad campaign, **click here.** And to pitch in to stop them, **click here.**

SUBJECT LINE: Expose automaker's deception

The third email, called "last chance," updated recipients on the amount of money still needed, and offered them one last chance to participate.

Union of Concerned Scientists
Citizens and Scientists for Environmental Solutions

LAST CHANCE!

Expose Auto Alliance Deception

Dear Madeline,

Our campaign to stop the Auto Alliance, the lobbyist group representing most major automakers, from running deceptive ads that claim "Autos manufactured today are virtually emission-free" is getting noticed far and wide-thanks to your generous response. Our first ad placement in RollCall.com has already generated "buzz" in Washington, and then just this Tuesday it was the subject of a feature story in the New York Times!

As a result of more than 20,000 inquiries (thank you for taking action!), the Federal Trade Commission is already evaluating the deceptive automakers' ad. And 568 people like you have helped the Union of Concerned Scientists raise an impressive $20,455.55 to put our counter ad in front of the industry and political leaders.

Now, we're ready to double our efforts to make sure the Auto Alliance's attempted deception is exposed so widely that automakers cannot hope to merely "weather the storm." With your help, we can raise another $20,000 in just one week so we can advertise not only in places the Auto Alliance did, but nationwide in publications automakers use to try and paint a green reputation. We need to build on our success quickly, so this is your last chance to help us make it happen. Click here to pitch in.

IF TODAY'S CARS ARE 'VIRTUALLY EMISSION FREE'...

...THEN SO IS THIS CIGARETTE.

LAST CHANCE to help us place our response ad above to expose the AutoAlliance's false claims. Let's build on our success and double the pressure!

If 570 supporters donate $35 by midnight on March 31, we can do it. Click here.

As you know, the Auto Alliance's advertising campaign is outrageous and we simply cannot let them get away with it. They are essentially telling our nation's lawmakers that their "job is done" and further emission regulations would be unneeded burdens on an environmentally responsible industry. However, today's cars, trucks, minivans and SUVs are emitting more global warming pollution than they did 20 years ago.

That's why we're fighting back with our counter ad. We have just a few more days to raise the necessary funds to ensure that our ad gets maximum visibility. If only 570 more supporters donate $35 each, we're there. We'll be able to stop the Auto Alliance from continuing misrepresentations that are harmful to consumers, the environment, and public health. Simply click here to make an online contribution to underwrite placement of the ads.

Thank you for participating in this important effort to make sure Congress and consumers know that pollution from new cars, trucks, and SUVs is still a major problem that cannot be ignored or covered up.

Thank you,

Kevin Knobloch
President

P.S. To learn more about the auto industry's false ad campaign, click here. And to pitch in to stop them, click here.

SUBJECT LINE: Automaker deception makes news - keep the pressure on

The fourth and final email thanked constituents (this was in addition to the auto-response message generated when they donated or took action). The message was heartfelt and detailed, honoring the recipient's interest and action.

Union of Concerned Scientists
Citizens and Scientists for Environmental Solutions

THANK YOU!

Expose Auto Alliance Deception

Dear Madeline,

Thank you! We're overwhelmed by the outpouring of activism and generosity you demonstrated in telling the Auto Alliance that you will not stand by while they mislead the public.

When we first came to you with news of the Auto Alliance's false advertising and our plan to counter it, we weren't sure what to expect. We quickly found out! You sprang into action, flooding the FTC with over 24,000 requests to open an investigation. Within days we received a letter from the FTC saying, *"The communications we have received are already more than ample to allow us to begin evaluating the substance of the complaints."* While we still await final word on the investigation, there is no denying that they heard you, loud and clear.

Then, when we came to you to ask for help in placing our ad to counter the Auto Alliance's misleading advertisement, you responded more strongly than we ever could have dreamed. The results: 1,100 individual contributions totaling over $40,000 have already allowed us to put our ad online with the influential Capitol Hill news source, RollCall.com. We've also purchased keywords on Google and Yahoo tied to phrases that the auto industry closely monitors for its own market and image.

And there's more: this week, as Congress returns from recess to begin consideration of a comprehensive Energy Bill, we will run our ad in the two major Capitol Hill newspapers - *Roll Call* and National Journal's *Congress Daily - AND* deliver a full-color print version of our ad and fact sheet to every single Senator and member of Congress, along with letters to key Congressional staff. Combine that with expanding our online ad presence to a number of the top news sites and blogs on the internet... and we'll reach a bigger audience than we ever could have dreamed. Thank you.

In the meantime, the Auto Alliance has remained publicly resolute on this issue... commenting in an auto trade press article that *"they will not stop using [the ads]."* But we have heard from a number of different sources that individual automakers are reconsidering this ad campaign, and have, to this date, stopped running the ads in the Washington, DC media they had been saturating before.

In other words, thanks to your actions and generous contributions, the Auto Alliance is now well aware that their misrepresentations will not go unchallenged. We will continue to push auto companies to play a constructive role in cleaning up vehicle emissions, but when they attempt an end run around the facts, we will expose their deceptive practices to decision makers and consumers.

To stay updated on this campaign and all our work to protect our planet and improve the health and safety our environment, visit our **Action Center**.

Thank you again for your contributions to this successful campaign,

Kevin Knobloch
President

SUBJECT LINE: Thanks for your support

The results

This campaign more than tripled the returns of any previous online campaign by the Union of Concerned Scientists. The table below shows the full results.

Segment	Segment size	# gifts	Response rate	Total donated	Avg gift
Donors	25,053	405	1.62%	$15,767	$38.95
Prospects	100,982	954	.95%	$32,947	$34.54
Total	126,035	1,359	1.08%	$48,714	$35.85

• Campaign No. 3 – Matching gift

An online matching gift is a perfect example of how email's marriage of affordability and urgency yields wonderful results. Even if yours is a small email list, it will usually do well with this approach. Messages will be forwarded, responded to, and generate new revenue.

A few years back, the nation's leading gay and lesbian advocacy organization, the Human Rights Campaign (HRC), discovered just how successful a matching gift can be.

Prior to this time, HRC was like many national membership organizations with a respectable email list generating decent returns. But then the issue of same-sex marriage was catapulted onto front pages across the country.

Almost overnight, HRC's email list grew exponentially (and hasn't slowed much since). Recall what I said in Chapter Two about large lists. They look good but usually they contain a high percentage of marginally engaged people. That could describe HRC's list, which is why the results of their online matching gift campaign wowed us all.

The campaign consisted of three emails: the first introduced the fundraising campaign, the second gave recipients a second chance to give, and the third said thank you.

Shown below, the first email explained the opportunity. A major donor had offered to match contributions dollar-for-dollar. It helped that HRC was in the news at the time, adding juice to an already strong ask.

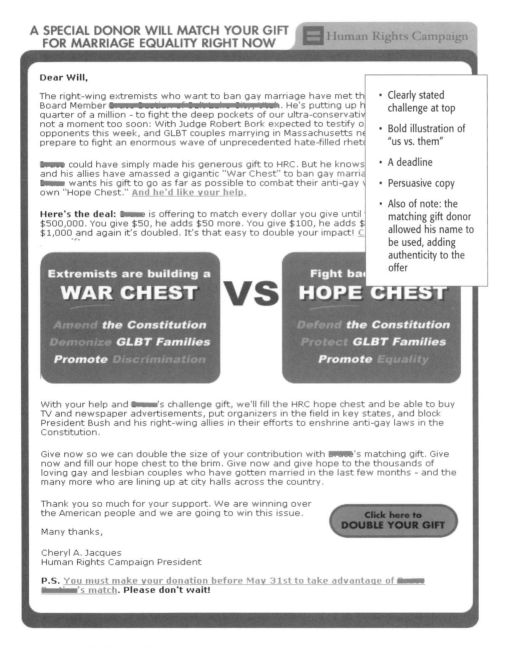

A SPECIAL DONOR WILL MATCH YOUR GIFT FOR MARRIAGE EQUALITY RIGHT NOW

Human Rights Campaign

Dear Will,

The right-wing extremists who want to ban gay marriage have met th... Board Member ████████████████████████. He's putting up h... quarter of a million - to fight the deep pockets of our ultra-conservativ... not a moment too soon: With Judge Robert Bork expected to testify o... opponents this week, and GLBT couples marrying in Massachusetts ne... prepare to fight an enormous wave of unprecedented hate-filled rhet...

████ could have simply made his generous gift to HRC. But he knows... and his allies have amassed a gigantic "War Chest" to ban gay marria... ████ wants his gift to go as far as possible to combat their anti-gay ... own "Hope Chest." <u>And he'd like your help.</u>

Here's the deal: ████ is offering to match every dollar you give until ... $500,000. You give $50, he adds $50 more. You give $100, he adds $... $1,000 and again it's doubled. It's that easy to double your impact! C...

- Clearly stated challenge at top
- Bold illustration of "us vs. them"
- A deadline
- Persuasive copy
- Also of note: the matching gift donor allowed his name to be used, adding authenticity to the offer

Extremists are building a
WAR CHEST
Amend **the Constitution**
Demonize **GLBT Families**
Promote *Discrimination*

VS

Fight ba...
HOPE CHEST
Defend **the Constitution**
Protect **GLBT Families**
Promote *Equality*

With your help and ████'s challenge gift, we'll fill the HRC hope chest and be able to buy TV and newspaper advertisements, put organizers in the field in key states, and block President Bush and his right-wing allies in their efforts to enshrine anti-gay laws in the Constitution.

Give now so we can double the size of your contribution with ████'s matching gift. Give now and fill our hope chest to the brim. Give now and give hope to the thousands of loving gay and lesbian couples who have gotten married in the last few months - and the many more who are lining up at city halls across the country.

Thank you so much for your support. We are winning over the American people and we are going to win this issue.

Click here to DOUBLE YOUR GIFT

Many thanks,

Cheryl A. Jacques
Human Rights Campaign President

P.S. <u>You must make your donation before May 31st to take advantage of ████ ████'s match</u>. **Please don't wait!**

SUBJECT LINE: A special donor will double your donation today

Shown below is the second and final ask of the series (the third email, as I mentioned, was a thank you), HRC kept the same design as the first email. Even without reading the message, those who haven't given are reminded to do so.

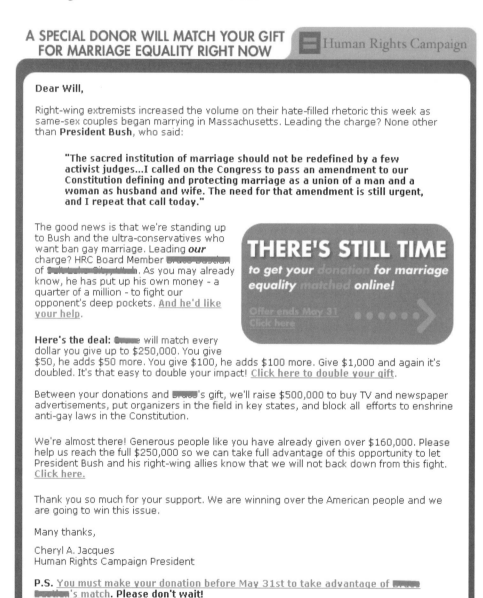

SUBJECT LINE: Respond to the attacks today and have your gift doubled

The results

Both of the emails asking for support did well, with 60 percent of the response coming from the first and 40 percent from the second. Overall the campaign generated nearly $300,000 in revenue, not counting the donor's matching gift. It added more than 3,000 people to HRC's donor list.

Segment	Segment size	# gifts	Response rate	Total donated	Avg gift
Donors	44,466	1,701	3.8%	$95,246	$55.99
Prospects	397,990	3,117	.08%	$189,794	$60.88
Total	442,456	4,818	1.08%	$285,040	$59.16

• Campaign No. 4 – Repetition of the same message

This is the easiest campaign of all!

Recently, I was part of an urgent campaign for a client. It was based on news that broke on the Friday morning of a three-day holiday weekend – hardly an ideal time as many people had left for vacation. But, the urgency of the news warranted our launching the email that same afternoon.

Over the weekend, we sent the *exact same email* a second time, suppressing those who had given to the first message.

And on the Tuesday after the holiday weekend, we sent the third email – again, *the exact same message.*

That's right: we sent the identical email three times. The only difference was that on the second and third, we added a brief message at the top:

As one of (Organization's) most important supporters, I'm re-sending you this urgent message. Because the news came on the Friday of a holiday weekend, many people missed it – and that means we're already losing time in this fight.

The results

Surprisingly, there were only a handful of complaints from people who received the three emails.

Further, the response rate from the people who received all three was a remarkable 2.5 percent.

I'm not recommending you do this regularly (it could start to get on people's nerves). But you might try it occasionally and see how it works for you.

•••

To be sure, there are more types of campaigns to launch than I've described here. In fact, the possibilities are nearly limitless.

What is important to remember – and it's the central message of this chapter – is this. While a single-shot email is sometimes successful, you will in most cases achieve better results with a three- or four-message campaign. More people will see your message; the importance of your objective will be reinforced; and, because your constituents have several chances to give, your returns will almost certainly be higher.

5

Compose Yourself

As far as email copy is concerned, there are two key writing components. The first is the subject line; the second is the body of the email itself. Since readers encounter the subject line first, let's begin there.

■ The scoop on subject lines

Talk about time being of the essence! To capture your constituents' attention and convince them that of the many emails bombarding their in-box, yours is the one they *must* read, you have a grand total of ... one to two seconds!

With that in mind, let's address a few subject line fundamentals:

• Length. Email programs vary as to how many characters your reader will see. Be on the safe side and limit your subject line to 50 characters.

• Shouting symbols ($, !, CAPS, *) and words such as: Free, Sale, Teens will land you in the spam filter. Avoid them. (Stay up to date on the "words to avoid' list by visiting: www.emailsherpa.com or www.clickz.com).

■ Tell, tease, take action

Depending on the situation, you'll speak in different voices with your subject line. For example, if your issue is timely, and your relationship with the donor is well-established, your job may simply be to "tell" him or her what is happening. Here's what I mean:

• A crisis occurs overseas and a relief agency sends an email letting donors know how they can help: "Send a blanket to Bamgarian flood victims."

• The "telling" approach also holds true for e-mails that help your users take care of business: "Order your Golf Gala tickets now," or "Your membership expires soon - renew today."

• Messages with time-sensitive content fall into the "telling" category as well: "Six vegan-friendly ways to decorate Easter eggs," delivered a few days before the holiday.

However, you won't always have straightforward opportunities to "tell" the facts. Here's when a little "teasing" is needed to get your reader's attention:

• An email landed in my box last week with this subject line: "The movie President Bush doesn't want you to see." That provocative approach works for me … I want to find out just what that movie is.

• Another way to tease is by being a bit clever. Quick, easy-to-scan clever:

"It's beginning to look a lot like justice..." sent just before the Christmas holidays by Earthjustice.

Lastly, whether you're telling or teasing, it's always important to use your subject line to call your readers to action. After all, nothing happens (i.e. sending you a donation, filling out a petition) until they take the next step.

The best "take action" emails are:

- Specific. Rather than exhort readers to "Tell them no",
  say instead: "Tell Big Tobacco to stop selling to children."

- Well-timed. Ideally, the topic is in the news.

- Local, if possible. "Tell Big Tobacco to stop selling
  to Boston children."

Once you've motivated your constituents to open your email, it's critical to give them something good to read.

■ Composing an email – Four elements

Writing good email messages starts with the basics of writing good copy, period. You must have a story to tell, offer a compelling reason to give, and use clear and persuasive language. Only a few key elements distinguish email copy from other forms of writing:

1) Make your email scannable

How do you read your own email? Do you pore over every word? Of course not. Neither do your constituents. If you're like most people, you tend to scan rather than read your messages. Therefore make sure your message is "scannable." That means:

- Short sentences
- Short paragraphs
- Numerous links to your donation page
- Graphic insets telling your reader what to do

• Bullets

• Selective use of bold and italics (reserve underlining for hyperlinks only)

Using these guidelines, your goal is to create a persuasive message that, in seven seconds or so, tells your constituent exactly what to do.

2) Keep it simple and short

In a direct mail fundraising letter, you have pages (sometimes as many as eight!) to let your story unfold. Not so with email!

Chances are good your constituents are a bit overwhelmed by the volume of email they receive, and a windy email from you will only add to the deluge. Keeping your message short and to the point is a service to your recipients. That means:

• Presenting only one or two key points

• Using as few words as possible to state your case

• Avoiding the history of your appeal (this is no time for background info)

3) Be aware of "preview panes"

Many of your readers won't get past the part of your email visible in their "preview panes." Shown on the next page is an email I recently received from The Humane Society of the United States.

Note how the issue and the ask are prominent in the first few sentences. You needn't read any further to grasp the point of this email.

That first impression is critical to your success. Treat those top few inches of copy and design as precious real estate. Tell your whole story right there.

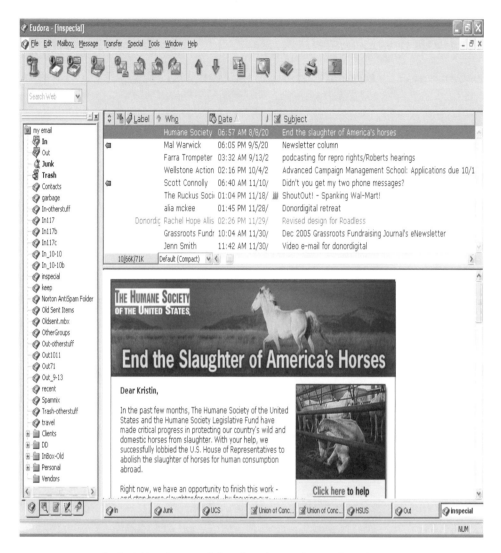

SUBJECT LINE: End the slaughter of America's horses

4) Keep the medium in mind

Email tends to be more casual than print. That means a more personal, less formal tone is appropriate and even expected. For example:

• Salutations and closings are typically more relaxed. A letter might begin with "Dear Ms. Stanionis," while an e-mail would start with "Hello Madeline."

• Email copywriters tend to use more colloquial terms. Direct mail copy might say, "We were truly overwhelmed by the generous response to our request." In email, that translates to, "Wow! You overwhelmed us (and that's hard to do)!"

• An up-to-the-minute style of writing is also appropriate. In direct mail language: "It was lovely to celebrate our anniversary with you last month." In email: "I'm writing this at midnight, just getting home after the anniversary party. Whew! What a night."

•••

In this chapter I've highlighted a few subtle ways in which writing email is different from other forms of writing. Still, good writing is good writing: specific, clear, and forceful. Email hasn't changed that a bit!

6

There's a Lot of Noise Out There

Consider your own email in-box. Just today. Overflowing? You're not alone. And that's why our job is hard and only getting harder. As the saying goes, "there's a lot of noise out there … you gotta be loud to be heard."

Already we've discussed several ways to amp up the volume of your email appeals. Conducting a campaign, rather than sending isolated messages, is one. Timing your emails smartly is another. And in the next chapter we'll discuss the importance (and profitability) of integrating email with your other fundraising channels.

These are all sound strategies, but none can stand alone without one other vital element: your ability to create that certain something that prompts your constituent to look twice, forward your email to a friend, perhaps mention it around the office … and make his or her own gift, of course.

How do you talk about something as ephemeral as creativity? You don't. Or at least I don't. I'm not a psychologist or a philosopher. And

I'm not sure *talking* about it matters anyway.

So, instead, let's look at creativity in action, exploring how four very different organizations made their campaigns memorable.

• Example No. 1 – Political and pointed

Let's start with an email created to raise dollars *and* eyebrows for NARAL Pro-Choice America, the leading national advocate for personal privacy and a woman's right to choose.

This effort was quite simple: one email which offered recipients the chance to give President Bush a tongue-in-cheek birthday gift. It sported large, eye-catching graphics and short text.

What do you give the President who thinks he should have everything?

How about a reality check -- from America's pro-choice majority!

President Bush's birthday is July 6. Thanks to anti-choice leaders in Congress, he's gotten a little TOO much of what he's asked for lately. So we've got the perfect gift: a birthday card from you, compliments of NARAL Pro-Choice America!

<u>Donate to NARAL Pro-Choice America today</u>, and we'll give President Bush your best birthday present -- a piece of your mind!

Best of all, your donation goes toward protecting the very rights he wants to take away and will help ensure that a woman's right to choose remains private, safe and legal.

SUBJECT LINE: Bush's birthday's coming up: send him the perfect gift!

Was the email successful? You bet it was. It drew a one-percent response, resulting in more than $35,000 in just a few days. Roughly half of the gifts were from first-time donors. And thanks to its creativity, 15 percent of the gifts came from people who didn't receive the original email, but heard about it from a friend.

Why it worked

In my opinion, this effort was successful for at least four reasons:

• *Visual impact.* Sharp and startling images, including the President holding a bold sign that made the case quickly and pointedly.

• *Recognizable theme.* In one way or another, we've all puzzled over what to give someone who seems to have everything.

• *Brevity.* The text was short and to the point. While not always the rule, shorter is usually better.

• *A receptive list.* NARAL Pro-Choice America constituents are responsive to daring political statements and this email speaks to the issues they care about.

One important caveat: Using political humor in which the President or other political figure is the target can be controversial, and you certainly risk alienating a segment of your file. In this instance, NARAL's capable donor relations team handled the small number of negative comments quickly.

Example No. 2 – A gimmick that worked

A few years ago, Environmental Defense ran the "Undo It" campaign to pass the McCain-Lieberman Climate Stewardship Act, legislation that would have among other things placed firm caps on greenhouse gas emissions. To raise money for the effort, the agency created the "51 Club," named for the number of votes needed in the Senate to pass the bill – and for the dollar amount requested.

To achieve maximum impact, Environmental Defense integrated the '51 Club' campaign into all of its fundraising channels – online, telemarketing, direct mail – and ran the campaign for six weeks.

Online, the campaign consisted of six emails, although most of the 240,000 recipients received no more than four.

The message

The first email, shown on the next page, set the tone for the campaign (all subsequent messages were similar except that they contained updated news and progress).

Look closely and you'll see that Environmental Defense used several smart techniques. First, by displaying an image of the writer, their well-known executive director, the organization helped foster a more personal connection. "This is no bureaucracy" was the underlying implication.

Second, a graphic box describing how contributions would be used made the appeal concrete. Five specific ways were cited.

Lastly, a goal and a familiar thermometer showed readers at a glance how progress was going.

The results

In six weeks, the campaign generated more than $725,000 from all fundraising channels, about a quarter of the gifts coming in online.

Overall, the campaign achieved a .25 percent response rate from the entire list, with more engaged segments clocking in at more than one percent. The first and last messages in the six-part series performed the best.

Why it worked

In my view, the campaign was successful for a number of reasons:

e
ENVIRONMENTAL DEFENSE
ACTION FUND

GLOBAL WARMING
UNDO IT.
We have an historic opportunity.

TO: Madeline Stanionis
FR: Fred Krupp
RE: Urgent Mobilization to Pass McCain-Lieberman Climate Stewardshp Act

Contribute $51 and join the 51 Club.

I have just learned that the second vote on the McCain-Lieberman Climate Stewardship Act has been scheduled in the U.S. Senate for as soon as mid-May and I urgently need your help to ramp up our campaign to win this major environmental victory. Global warming is the most urgent environmental problem facing the world today, and McCain-Lieberman is the most comprehensive and practical approach to cutting America's global warming pollution.

Help us reach our goal
$725,000 by June 1st

$294,163 raised as of 5/18/04

$51 $375,000 $725,000

51 CLUB

GIVE NOW ▶

We have precious little time to mobilize and raise the funds necessary to battle powerful special interests in Washington who are opposed to McCain-Lieberman.

In the few weeks we have before the vote, we must raise at least $725,000 if we are to have the resources necessary to win this historic vote.

That's why I am inviting you to become a member of the 51 Club today. The sole purpose of the 51 Club is to raise the financial resources necessary to mobilize the American people to win 51 votes in the Senate to pass the McCain-Lieberman Act. With 51 votes, we will have a global warming majority in the Senate for the first time ever.

To join, I need you to do one simple thing:

* Send $51 or more to finance this urgent campaign

As a 51 Club member you will receive weekly campaign updates from the field on how your support is making a difference in this historic fight for the future of our planet.

We don't have a moment to lose. Please act today.

Thank you.

Fred Krupp

PS: Every dollar will help us win this critical vote. If you can give more than $51 please consider doing so. If less, know that I appreciate whatever you can do.

About the 51 Club

Your contribution will help to:

* Fire up grassroots efforts in 5 swing states—Tennessee, Arkansas, Louisiana, Ohio and Nebraska

* Get 500,000 Emissions Petition signatures before the Senate vote

* Flood the media with our message: tv, radio, newspaper and Internet.

* Boost our Capitol Hill lobbying efforts

* Get a 51-vote majority in the Senate to pass the Climate Stewardship Act

$ **GIVE NOW** ▶

What are the senators saying?

"Over time, we will win. The scientific evidence is on our side. We will win."
- Senator John McCain (R-AZ)

"A growing chorus of voices is demanding that we act to address global warming. With such a groundswell, the day of action is coming. Together, we can take another big step toward that action this spring."
- Senator Joe Lieberman (D-CT)

📋 **SIGN THE PETITION** ▶

SUBJECT LINE: Urgent mobilization to undo global warming

- The *offer* – 51 votes, $51 gift – was catchy. It stuck with you.

- The emails were *visually compelling* and different from Environmental Defense's other online appeals.

- *Persistence*. Environmental Defense delivered a sustained campaign.

- A *good list*. As usual, without a good list the campaign would have floundered.

Example No. 3 – Warm and clever

Heifer International is among the most well-known Internet success stories. Their mission to end hunger and poverty appeals to a broad spectrum of people. The vast majority of their online income comes in via web traffic near the end of the year – likely, people who received their direct mail appeal who come online to make their gift.

While Heifer had used email to generate gifts at other times throughout the year, the agency hadn't tried Thanksgiving. This relatively simple, one-time email, shown on the next page, was a bit of a test.

The message

Seeking to communicate a positive way to remember those in need, the email was upbeat and pretty. It featured a visually interesting list of how the reader could help make Thanksgiving a little more special, for themselves and for families around the world.

The underlying message: it won't take a great sacrifice on your part to help those who are hungry. One or two little actions will mean a lot.

The results

The campaign generated healthy results from their e-mail list.

Help Heifer Fill Their Plates

Dear Madeline,

With the holiday season around the corner, you're probably already planning festivities with your family around an abundant dinner table. This year, consider adding one more tradition to your list: filling the plates of families in other countries while you fill your own. Click here.

Did you know that in most 2nd and 3rd world countries, a holiday family meal might consist of as little as a few potatoes, carrots and rice? The contrast between your holiday meal and theirs is pretty dramatic. But it doesn't have to be this way. Here's how you can make this year's holidays just a little more special – for you, and for families around the world.

LIGHTEN YOUR WORK LOAD.
When you're making your shopping list, consider dropping an item or two from your planned menu. Maybe you could serve just one pie or leave a bottle of wine off your holiday list.

FILL THE PLATE.
Use the money that would have been spent on that extra dish to make a gift to a hungry family. Purchase a flock of chicks to provide eggs, goats to provide milk, even bees to provide honey through Heifer International's "Most Important Gift Catalog in the World." Not only will your gift provide critical nutrition for a meal, but your sacrifice means a family in need will have meals all year round.

EDUCATE.
At your holiday feast, take a minute to tell your family about what you're **not** serving for dinner – and why. The holidays are a perfect time to be reminded of just how much we have to be thankful for.

SPREAD THE WORD.
Lighten a friend's workload and fill even more plates by sharing this e-mail. Click here.

Thank you for your generosity this holiday season. I hope you'll make this a holiday to remember and browse our gift catalog today.

Wishing you a warm and loving holiday,

Jill Bayles
Heifer International

SUBJECT LINE: Make your holiday mean meaningful - 4 easy steps!

Moreover, it didn't appear that the Thanksgiving appeal hurt Heifer's year-end holiday giving program.

Why it worked

In my opinion, here's why this one-shot email worked:

• *The contrast* between haves and have-nots was starkly presented without being depressing.

• *Easy-to-follow steps* such as "Lighten your work load" and "Fill the plate" made the email easy to read and the offer easy to grasp.

• *The message treated donors personally* by understanding their daily lives – shopping for dinner, wanting to have meaningful conversations with family, and being overwhelmed with tasks during the holidays.

•••

Sure, it's easy for me to say, "Be creative!" It's just as easy for you to break out in a cold sweat.

Certainly, if you are creative, or can tap someone who is, your emails stand a greater chance of succeeding (assuming yours is a compelling cause, of course). But there's another quality that rivals creativity, one that produces more impressive results. And you're blessed with it yourself.

As you saw in Chapter 2 with the email sent by the Massachusetts Society for the Prevention of Cruelty to Animals, speaking from the heart is a powerful force. Mesmerizing even. You know from your own experience how the moment seems to stop when a friend or family member bares their soul.

Keep this in mind as you struggle – or even obsess – about the nuances of design or copy. Those are important, yes. But also remember your mother's admonishment on your first day of middle school: be yourself! You'll be amply rewarded.

7

The Sum of Your Parts

Imagine this scenario:

Just after Thanksgiving, your donor receives your organization's year-end holiday card in the mail. Since you've chosen a particularly nice image, she keeps the card on her mantle.

A week later, she receives your letter asking her to make a year-end gift – she sets it aside to take care of later. In the holiday commotion, she simply forgets about it.

Then, days before the year ends, your email lands in her in-box with the same graphic theme as your card, offering a last chance to make a tax-deductible gift this year. The familiar image catches her eye and the copy reminds her of her good intention. She makes a gift.

Finally, just after the New Year, she receives a call thanking her for her gift, and wishing her a happy new year.

Direct response professionals might refer to this integration of communication channels as the "Holy Grail." Donors receive messages that reinforce and repeat each other in a variety of fundraising channels, making it easy for them to give.

Does it work?

Will integrating your website and email campaigns with your direct mail and telemarketing programs raise more money? Based on my experience, the answer is a resounding "Yes." Familiarity in this case breeds results.

To illustrate *why* integration works, let's look more closely at the example above. Four elements are important to note:

• By repeating the image from the holiday card, and the copy from the direct mail appeal, the email this donor received served to *remind* her about the need, rather than introduce and sell her on a new concept.

• Each medium – direct mail, telephone, and e-mail – did what it does best. Direct mail offered a holiday card and a traditional letter. Email was used for urgency – a last minute gift. And the telephone delivered a personal, warm message.

• Each medium delivered the right message for your donor's previous action. Had she responded to the letter, you wouldn't have sent the email. And had your donor not given to the e-mail, your phone call might have been used to ask for a gift.

• The cohesion of all your media assured the donor that yours is a serious and well-organized group.

Would that we could all follow this seemingly simple process!

To get you started on integrating your own fundraising channels, I've developed a five-step program for renewing your donors. Let's look at each step now.

1) Put together a calendar

This is relatively simple. Look at your direct mail and telemarketing schedule and plug in the online opportunities as shown in this calendar. I've italicized the online components:

January

1st-10th	New year telemarketing calls
5th	Renewal 1 direct mail drops
12th-19th	*Renewal home page hi-jack (explanation of this term to follow)*
Jan 15	*Renewal 1 post email sent*

February

10th	*Renewal 2 pre-email sent*
25th	Renewal 2 direct mail drops

March

10th	*Pre-Telemarketing email sent*
22nd-29th	Renewal telemarketing calls

April

1st	Renewal 3 direct mail drops
10th	*Renewal 3 post email sent*

May

10th	*Renewal 4 pre-email sent*
15th	Renewal 4 direct mail drops

August

1st	Last chance renewal direct mail drops
22nd	*Last chance renewal post email sent*

You may have noticed that not every effort is integrated. It's difficult for even the most sophisticated online fundraisers to integrate everything, and sometimes it doesn't make sense. For example, special appeals online and offline are usually quite different. Online appeals tend to reflect late-breaking news more closely than direct mail appeals. And, obviously, you can't predict such news opportunities.

2) Develop copy and layout for your integrated emails

Ever bought an airline ticket online? Tickets to a play? Of course you have. What do you like best about it? How poetic the ticket options sound or how attractively the flight options were displayed? Of course not. You simply like that you can take care of business quickly and easily.

Remember this when you design your online renewal messages.

Some of your donors are going online to take care of their *philanthropy* business. Make it quick and easy. Forget through-the-roof creative. Your goal isn't to dazzle, it's to get results.

As for wording your renewal emails, there are three options to choose from:

A) Repeat your direct mail renewal letter, word-for-word, in your email. However, because of your letter's length, this isn't a very practical solution.

B) Create a new message based on the overall theme of the mail piece. This doesn't make sense either given how you've worked on the direct mail copy.

C) Edit your renewal letter for a shorter e-mail version. This is the preferred choice, since you have the copy to work with and can incorporate the same color and graphics if needed.

3) Segment your list

The typical way to segment your list is obvious: by previous giving level. This allows you to ask donors to renew at a level equal to or greater than their previous gift. Your grouping might look like this:

• Segment 1) Donors whose previous gift was $1-$34

- Segment 2) Donors whose previous gift was $35-$59
- Segment 3) Donors whose previous gift was $60-$99
- Segment 4) Donors whose previous gift was $100-$249
- Segment 5) Donors whose previous gift was $250 and above

A more recent twist is to further segment by those who have given online. This can be quite a cost saver, allowing you to suppress these donors from your regular mail file if their giving history shows they are giving online repeatedly.

4) Determine if you'll send your email messages before or after a letter or phone call

As you'll note in the calendar, sometimes I say "pre-email" and at other times "post email." Is it better to email before or after a direct mail or telemarketing effort? I'd like to say one performs better, but I can't make that claim … at least not yet. So I tend to do a combination of both pre- and post email messages.

- *Pre-emails.* It's ideal to launch a pre-email and get the results in time to suppress those donors from the other channel. Typically that means sending your email up to 10 days prior to your other effort.

- *Post emails.* Given the challenges of predicting bulk mail delivery dates, I tend to do more post emails. There's less room for error. Typically I'll send the email about a week or two after the letter arrives.

5) Remember to include your website

The calendar I outlined doesn't account for one key element: Whenever you drop a mail piece or run a telemarketing campaign, expect some donors to give via your website (whether you asked them to or not).

For this reason, always provide a specific web address on your mail pieces and offer it to those you call. But don't leave it at that. Place a prominent graphic on your site so that donors know just where to click to renew their gift. Don't make them guess.

•••

There you have it: a relatively simple process for integrating your renewal program into your direct mail and telemarketing channels. If it's too aggressive for your tastes, modify it. Instead of sending several emails before or after your letter hits, maybe you send one.

What's most important now, if you're new to online renewals, is to get your feet wet. Start learning what works and what doesn't for your organization. As you gain confidence, you can always (and I predict you will) expand your efforts.

■ The Human Rights Campaign renewal series

A gay and lesbian advocacy group, the Human Rights Campaign has a large, loyal, and Internet-savvy constituency. HRC's renewal drive illustrates many of the integration elements we just discussed.

The success of HRC's campaign is due to many reasons, among them are cleanly designed pages, well-placed links, messages and graphics that reinforce one another, and sheer persistence – HRC sends out emails frequently.

I want to call your attention to three particular pieces.

1) Home page hijack

You noticed in the sample calendar the term, *"Renewal home page hijack."* This simply means that, for a brief period, an organization *replaces* its regular home page with one devoted to acquiring and renewing memberships.

The time to do this is when you send your *first* direct mail and email seeking renewals (typically this first one draws the best response). Many of the recipients will head to your site to renew, so it makes sense to feature your renewal drive on your home page.

Shown here, HRC's 'hijack' page makes it easy to renew and, just as importantly, offers *anyone* visiting the site the opportunity to join.

Those who clicked on the RENEW link were taken to the donation page shown on the next page.

It reinforced the renewal message, and was quite simple – free of links or promotions. There was little to distract the donor from his or her mission of making a gift.

While not shown here, HRC preprinted the name and address fields and also pre-selected the $50 gift level. Many donors will note the level and often increase their commitment.

2) Renewal email message sent after a direct mail piece arrived

The next message shown below was sent about a week after HRC's direct mail hit. It's what I referred to in the calendar as a "post email". Note the similarity in look to the first email, and how it serves to 'remind' readers of the previous one.

SUBJECT LINE: Renew your HRC membership

3. Renewal email message sent prior to a telemarketing call

Lastly, the "pre-email" shown next is a favorite of mine. It had dual objectives. On the one hand, HRC was implicitly inviting members to renew prior to their being called. On the other hand, for those who didn't renew at this point, HRC was preparing them for the call. Everybody won: members who wanted a phone call, those who didn't,

Dear Will,

Our team is about to start working the phones for the Human Rights Campaign Annual Membership Drive, and we're hoping to reach you soon (probably in a month or two). Phone calls have always been a great way for us to keep in touch with you on important GLBT issues — and there is certainly so much to talk about right now.

As you know, last month same-sex couples began getting married in Massachusetts and became living examples of marriage equality. In response to these celebrations of commitment, President Bush renewed his commitment to work with the ultra-conservatives who are behind the anti-gay, anti-family Constitutional Amendment. With a Senate vote scheduled for early July, we cannot rest. Our efforts to fight any discriminatory amendment and to support candidates in November who will champion equality have never been more important. We're looking forward to hearing your thoughts about this critical battle when we call you to renew your HRC membership.

Of course, if you'd prefer not to wait for a phone call to renew, it's easy to take care of your membership gift online. **Renewing online** is completely secure, and saves us the cost of phoning, so more of your gift goes towards our important work right away. **Simply click here** or paste this URL into your browser window:
https://secure.qa3.org/03/renew_tm/nZ7_SslK14a0r??source=WO5CGERG1

CLICK HERE TO ·····>
Renew Online Today

There's never been a more amazing — and challenging — time to **renew your Human Rights Campaign membership**. From the joyous weddings in Massachusetts to the ballot box in November, the center of our community's historic and heartening struggle for full equality under the law is you.

Thank you in advance for remaining true to our fight for equality with your renewed membership gift.

Many thanks,

Ann Crowley,
Deputy Development Director for Annual Giving & Membership Outreach

P.S. If you've already renewed your HRC membership, THANK YOU, and please forgive this gentle reminder.

If you would like to unsubscribe from a specific Human Rights Campaign list, or update your account settings, you can visit your Subscription Management Page. Click here to remove yourself from all Human Rights Campaign lists.

SUBJECT LINE: Calling on you to renew your commitment

and HRC who gave them the choice.

●●●

In closing this chapter, I must confess that creating a cohesive, well-timed set of emails – usually requiring a number of people to work cooperatively – is a pain in the neck, enough to give you pause or even discourage you.

Still, it's critical to strive toward integration. The dollars bear it out. Of the organizations I work with, those that blend their fundraising channels are raising the most money – online and offline.

Recall the example I gave at the beginning of the chapter where direct mail, telemarketing, and email all complemented one another. You just can't beat the efficiency of it all.

8

What to Send
When You're Not Soliciting

So far, we've discussed email as it pertains to fundraising only. But your donors will quickly tire of your messages, and click delete, if all you do is ask for money.

If you expect to hold their interest – consistently – then your donors need to hear from you at other times too.

What should you be sending in between your email appeals? The answer is cultivation messages. All those good ideas we've discussed for clever, educational, and compelling messages can be put to excellent use in your effort to build relationships and bring your donors closer to you.

Typical cultivation efforts include the following:

• **E-newsletters.** Often, an e-newsletter is the first step in an organization's online communications strategy – and it's a good one, especially for groups not particularly active online. Keep in mind your online newsletter is *not* your print newsletter simply sent via email (or, yikes, as a PDF!). Rather, your e-newsletter should be visually interesting, contain fresh information, and be shorter and a little more casual and personal than your print version.

- **Ways to get involved.** Advocacy alerts, volunteer opportunities, events, and activities your constituents can do at home are often important parts of your mission – and great cultivation pieces, too.

- **Acknowledgments**. It's important after any campaign to send a wrap-up and thank you email. I'm not referring to a simple acknowledgment and receipt. I mean a more descriptive email describing what happened as a result of the campaign: "We achieved our goal, all the kids went to summer camp, and here are a few pictures." You can also use holidays (Thanksgiving is a prime example) or other special dates to acknowledge and thank donors out of the blue.

- **Issue updates.** What happened to the ocelots three months later? Your donors want to know! That's why they made a donation.

- **Fun stuff**. See Chapter Two. All the tactics used for list building (such as flash movies, ecards, surveys) are also great cultivators.

Lastly, a **Welcome series** is an effective cultivation tool, especially since response rates for those new to your email list tend to be higher. The following is an example from the Human Rights Campaign.

The first email, shown on the next page, was a personal message from the president and a guide to the HRC's online program. Note the personal nature of the email, featuring a photo of Joe Solmonese, and an unmistakable headline that sums up the purpose of this message.

Welcome!
I'm glad you're here.

A personal message from
HRC President Joe Solmonese

HUMAN RIGHTS CAMPAIGN®

Your guide to HRC online

Dear Will,

On behalf of all of us at the Human Rights Campaign, I'd like to welcome you to HRC online. At this moment in history, the Gay, Lesbian, Bisexual and Transgender (GLBT) community and all of our allies are fighting day in and day out for fairness in America. By becoming part of our online community, you have taken a critical first step in helping ensure that the voice of tolerance is heard in every part of the country. We hope that you'll take advantage of the many resources we have to offer and that you'll spend some time learning more about the work we do.

Most of all, I want you to know that your opinions and needs matter to us. That's why we are happy to offer a simple effective way to manage how we communicate with you. You can subscribe or unsubscribe to our e-newsletters, find out about our latest advocacy campaigns, and update your personal information with just a click of your mouse. **To manage or view your preferences online, click here.**

Again, I want to personally thank you for signing up as an HRC online activist. Your support is truly the foundation of our organization and we look forward to getting to know you!

Warmly,

Joe Solmonese
HRC President

PS - If at any time you'd like to drop us a line to let us know how we're doing, please feel free to contact us at field@hrc.org.

Most visited pages at hrc.org:

» **Get Local**
Find your state's latest status on GLBT issues and get involved with HRC in your community.

» **HRC Family Life**
Support and resources on parenting, adoption, domestic partner agreements and more.

» **HRC Work Life**
Is your workplace GLBT friendly? Find out how to make a difference in your own workplace and what companies are on our "A" list.

» **MillionForMarriage.org**
Sign our petition to show your support for marriage equality and find ways to help spread the word.

» **Become a member of HRC today. Click here.**

SUBJECT LINE: Welcome! I'm glad you're here

Shown below, the second welcome email from the Human Rights Campaign was a membership invitation sent within 60 days of the recipient's online registration. (I now recommend sending the

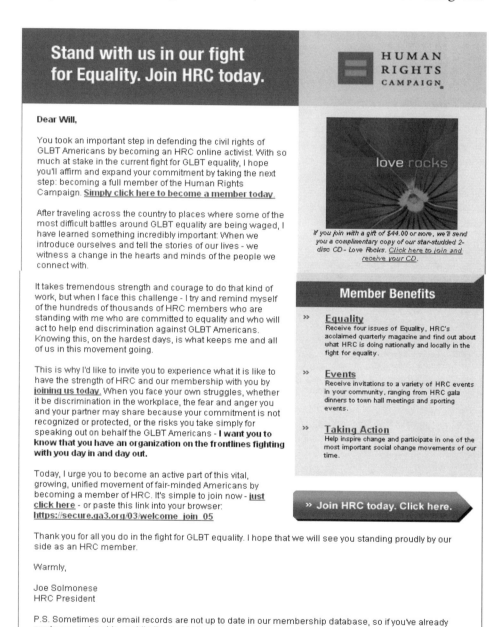

SUBJECT LINE: Fight for equality: Become a member

invitation much earlier – within a week of registration if possible).

The third in HRC's welcome series invited feedback, and garnered very high click-through rates (the number of people who clicked on

How are we doing?
Take our online survey

HUMAN RIGHTS CAMPAIGN

Dear Will,

Because you are the center of the amazing and challenging struggle that is upon us, we need YOU to help guide our online work for the future. We've posted a quick survey to help you give us this important feedback. **Click here.**

We are committed to providing the online actions and information that you want to help fight for gay, lesbian, bisexual and transgender equality - so you tell us: What are we doing right? What could we do better? Who are you and how can we represent your needs best?

We take your opinions and feedback to heart, and we are strongly committed to representing your beliefs and needs. Please, **click here to tell us what you're thinking.**

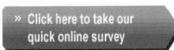

» **Click here to take our quick online survey**

Please note that the survey is anonymous. If you have a question or comment which requires a response, please e-mail us: **field@hrc.org.** Thanks in advance for taking a few minutes to give us your thoughts!

Warmly,

Joe Solmonese
Human Rights Campaign President

P.S. Can't see the clickable links? Paste this URL into your browser to take our survey: **http://www.surveymonkey.com/s.asp?u=91911519285**

SUBJECT LINE: How are we doing?

any link in the message).

■ Are we sending too much email?

Somewhere in between your e-newsletters, fundraising campaigns, event notices, action alerts, upgrades, and fun stuff, someone in your organization will raise the question: "Are we sending too much email?"

The answer? Maybe. Maybe not.

Organizations tend to raise the issue in response to either declining response rates or complaints from constituents. Both are important sources, and both are easily misunderstood.

The reality is, you probably can't answer the question. It's difficult to prove cause and effect, and rather than spend too much time mulling it over, I recommend arming yourself with facts and preparing solutions, per the following:

• **Larger lists produce more feedback** (obviously there are more people to hear from). So if you're emailing thousands or tens of thousands of people, you'll get your share of complaints, questions, and concerns. Though as a percentage the number will (usually) be small.

• **As a corollary, if your list is large, it probably contains a high number of those who are only marginally interested.** That only makes sense. You accept lower response rates if the revenue still justifies your effort.

• **Beware of low open rates – they may be false.** Open rates (the number of people who read your e-mail) have declined as a result of changing email program standards. More about this in the next chapter.

• **Review feedback over time.** Review your data on a monthly and quarterly basis to identify trends rather than be overly concerned with individual complaints or a bad week or responses here and there.

- **Aim high.** It's entirely possible you are sending too much email – or, rather, you're sending too much *bad* email. Use the concern to evaluate your program. I've found that once organizations begin emailing, everyone wants in on the act, resulting in wildly varying quality. Someone in your organization should be looking at the program as a whole, saying "no" to random and unprofessional emails.

- **Do what you can to mitigate the situation.** If as a percentage you're getting more complaints than before, or your response rates are dropping, these two tactics can sometimes stabilize the situation:

  - **"Love notes."** During high-volume times, put a note in your email that says something like:

    "Thank you for your patience with our frequent e-mails during this campaign. We know you can't always take action, but we know you want to stay informed and be involved when you can. Thank you!"

  - **Update and use persuasive unsubscribe language**. You may even change your unsubscribe language to fit the season, a twist on the method described in Chapter Seven.

    "To unsubscribe simply follow the instructions below. If you are unsubscribing because of our frequent emails, please know that summer is our busiest time! It's when we have many events and need the most help – it'll be slower during the rest of the year. We hope you'll stick with us."

9

It's All About the Data

Just as with other direct response methods, success with email fundraising is measured by response rates. What is different from direct mail and telemarketing, however, is that email allows us to track some new and useful numbers.

For example, good email messaging software can track results you're familiar with, such as who gave, how much, and to which package.

But email tracking also allows you to learn whether your prospects opened their email; if they clicked on the giving link, but didn't give; even the time of day they made their gifts.

What follows is a chart showing the data I usually look at. Don't worry if your results differ sharply from these figures. Our industry is young and you can expect results to vary dramatically from organization to organization, segment to segment, effort to effort.

■ The data – at a glance

Yes, I know it looks a little intimidating...

Message title	Subject	Type	Segment	Date
Appeal: Holiday 05-YearEnd #1-Donors	Will you help end animal cruelty?	Appeal	Donors	12/9/05

Day of Week	Time of day	#Sent	#Rec'd	Bounce%	#Opens	Open rate
Thursday	11 a.m.	9,705	9,594	1.14%	3,742	39%

#Unsub	Unsub%	#Unique clicks	%Unique clicks	#Gifts	%Give
34	0.35%	622	6.48%	220	2.29%

%First online gifts	%Conversion-giving	Total Revenue	Average Gift
31.5%	32.59%	$9,039	$41.09

■ The data – in detail

... But let's break it down, metric by metric.

Message title
Appeal: Holiday 05-Year-end #1-Donors

Message Title. The name you've given your message. Using descriptive names allows you to recognize at a glance what type of email you sent.

Subject
Will you help end animal cruelty?

Subject The subject line for the email. Spend time writing and rewriting this, as it will determine whether your email gets opened.

Type
Appeal

Type. Whether your email is an appeal, acquisition, or renewal.

Segment
Donors

Segment. The segment these results are for.

Date
12/9/05

Date. The date your email was sent.

Day of Week
Thursday

Day of week. Much has been written about ideal days for email response, with many claiming Mondays and Fridays are poor email days. However, recent research casts doubt on such theories.

Time of Day
11:00 a.m.

Time of day The exact time your e-mail was sent. I've seen studies showing that people tend to take care of their online transactions during two windows each day: 10:00 a.m. to noon and (a distant second) 7:00 p.m. to 9:00 p.m. While this applies to all transactions, not just charitable donations, it's wise to keep these windows in mind when sending your emails.

#Sent
9,705

Number Sent. The number of emails you attempted to send.

#Rec'd
9,594

Percent received. The number of emails actually delivered, including those going through a spam filter. All subsequent calculations use this number (rather than the full number sent).

Bounce%
1.14%

Bounce percentage. The number of emails that weren't delivered. There are two kinds of bounces. *Soft* bounces are usually the result of a full email box or temporary server problem (your email vendor will try to deliver these emails later). A hard bounce signifies there's no recipient with that name at the domain, or the domain doesn't exist.

Over time, your list will contain a growing number

of hard bounces. Keep that in check. Download the hard bounces periodically and have your staff correct obvious mistakes (name@aok.com instead of aol.com). You may even consider sending hard bouncing names to a data firm that will attempt to append the new e-mail address.

#Opens	Open rate
3.742	39%

Opens/Open rate. The number and percent of recipients who opened your email. Many factors can affect your open rates, including when you send your email, the subject line, and whose name shows as the sender of your message.

However, before you can focus on increasing your open rates, you must confront two obstacles that affect "deliverability."

The first has to do with images. Most email messaging systems place a one pixel, invisible image in your email and calculate open rates based on how many computers receive the image.

The problem is, many email programs today aren't downloading *any* images - unless directed to. So while many of your recipients might still read the *text* of your email, they're not counted as having opened it.

The second obstacle are spam programs, called "filters," that catch unwanted email using a variety of methods. You can often avoid such a filter by doing the following:

• Work with a reputable email messaging company that has experience navigating the technical details and working with the major Internet service providers to resolve problems.

• Respond to spam complaints and spam requests. That means someone should be checking the in-box daily to reply to requests that verify your legitimacy. And of course people who complain about being on your list should be removed.

• Ask recipients to add you to their lists of approved senders, often called "white" or "buddy" lists.

%Unsub	%Unsub
34	0.35%

Number and percentage of unsubscribers. The number and percentage of recipients who unsubscribed from your list as a result of this particular email. Don't worry too much about your unsubscribe rate unless it's close to or over one percent per message.

You can sometimes keep these rates low by tweaking your unsubscribe language: "If you'd like to unsubscribe, please click here. We hope you won't though! Even if you don't always have time to stay involved in our cause, every little bit helps. Thanks for sticking with us."

#Unique Clicks	%Unique Clicks
622	6.48%

Number and percentage of unique clicks. The number and percentage of recipients who clicked on any link in your email– often called "click-through rate." Note: appeals will typically generate relatively low clicks, around three percent. Emails containing an urgent call to action will sometimes elicit clicks of more than 12 percent.

#Gifts	%Give
220	2.29%

Number and percentage of gifts. The number and percentage of recipients who made a gift (the response rate, in other words).

%First online gifts
31.5%

Percentage of first-time online givers. The percentage of recipients making a gift to your organization, online, for the first time. The donors in this group may be offline donors or prospects.

Conversion to Giving
32.59%

Conversion to giving. The percentage of recipients who clicked to the donate page and then completed the transaction without closing, or "abandoning," the page. Conversion rates of 30 percent are good ... and hard to come by!

Total revenue
$9,039

Total revenue. The total revenue generated by this e-mail message.

Average gift
$41.09

Average gift. You'll find that average gift amounts are usually higher online than in other channels - sometimes even double.

■ What are good results?

Results vary wildly among organizations. But if pressed, let me again cite the numbers I gave in Chapter Two.

If you want your email to generate **10** gifts, then:

- (At least) **1,000** people need to **receive** your message
- (At least) **250** people need to **open** (aka READ) your email
- (At least) **50** people need to **click on the link** to your donation page

In which case your overall response rate would be a respectable one percent. And *that* is a very good result!

•••

Your numbers may look very different from what I've shown in this chapter. Again, this medium is young - there will be fluctuations - sometimes dramatically so. Rather than fret about low open rates, or poor click to donate numbers, step back and look at trends over the course of six months to a year. Those will be far more reliable numbers and they'll indicate where your program might need extra attention.

10

Making the Most of the Numbers

With three or four email campaigns under your belt, the time – and urge – will come to improve your results. As with your other fundraising channels, you'll want your emails to be as thoughtfully prepared as possible.

Different challenges await you here. "How much do I need to explain on my donation page?" "Yikes, my open rates are in the basement!" "No matter what I do, I can't get my response rate above one percent." "Should I say it's a renewal in the subject line?" "Is my list as bad as I think it is?"

You need answers!

This is where segmenting and testing come into play.

■ Segmenting

Segmenting your donors into like groups is an important way to understand your constituents and generate higher response rates and larger gifts – both online and in your direct mail and telemarketing programs.

Due to the high cost of mailing or calling your entire list, segmenting in your direct mail and telemarketing programs is a necessity. Not so with email. Sending your message far and wide doesn't cost any more than sending it to a narrowly-defined segment. Thus, it's easy to simply select "all" and launch.

But cost isn't the only reason to segment. Even small details, such as acknowledging the recipient's giving history, "Thank you for your past support," can help boost your relationship-building efforts, and help you learn more about how different segments of your list respond.

For example, one effective way for organizations who do advocacy to segment is by level of involvement. You want to do well with those who are most engaged, and find out what if anything will spur those who are least engaged.

In this case, constituents would be segmented as follows:

• Donors;
• Super-activists – those who have taken more than five online actions in the last six months;
• Activists – those who have taken one to four actions such as signing a petition or forwarding a message to a friend in the last six months;
• Lapsed activists – those who haven't taken action in the last six months; and
• Everyone else – those who have joined the list during the last six months, and others for whom you have limited information.

Segmenting in this way allows you to deliver a relevant message and a call to action that fits your constituent's previous behavior. Of course, it also allows you to track the results for each of these key groups to learn how they are responding and to subsequently send messages guaranteed to generate a response.

Other segmentation strategies include the following:

• **Giving level.** Segmenting based on your donors' highest previous contribution is critical. For example, for donors who have given up to $35, you would create a donation page on which the gift levels start at $40 so you can attempt to upgrade them to a higher level.

• **Campaign-based.** Based on the action a recipient of your email campaign has taken on the particular issue. The segmenting would look like this:

- Donors who have taken action (sent a letter to the Governor, for example)
- Donors who haven't taken action
- Non-donors who have taken action
- Non-donors, who haven't taken action

Segmenting in this way allows you to acknowledge a recipient's specific action (one small step in building further support). It also gives you the information you need to motivate the recipient to the next steps.

• **Recency.** Based on the supposition that people who have recently added their name to your e-mail list not only have correct addresses and other updated information but are also more excited about your cause – and will perform better than older names. Recency can also refer to how recently a constituent took an action or made a gift.

• **Source.** Harkening back to Chapter Two and the list-building strategies we discussed, looking at the source or the campaign where the recipient joined the list is key. If you segment by source, you can learn which sources generate the highest responses – and, of course, get more people from the highest-performing sources.

• **One-time and lapsed online donors.** As with direct mail, getting a second gift is challenging. Many people make their first online gift as a result of a disaster like Hurricane Katrina (and then disappear until the next calamity). Segmenting these first-time donors will help you determine what, if anything, is likely to motivate a second gift.

• **Active and inactive non-donors.** As you grow your email list, the majority of your list members will be comprised of non-donors. Active non-donors may be those who have completed a survey, attended an event, or otherwise engaged with your cause – all of which I hope you've coded. It's worth looking at this segment to determine what type of appeal might spur a first gift.

There you have seven relatively simple ways to segment your email list. Yes, they may seem a bit daunting at the moment, but, heck, so would tying your shoes if I gave you written instructions. Go slow if you must, simply group your donors by giving levels if you haven't already. That alone will pay off nicely. From there, you might even start to find this whole segmenting thing a bit enjoyable.

■ Testing

Once you've built your list and determined how best to segment your constituents, you can begin to test what works *within* each of these segments. Note that testing is nearly impossible to do without a large list (of at least several thousand). If that describes your organization, do read on. I'll focus here on a few of the common variables for you to experiment with.

• **Open rates.** As discussed in Chapter Eight, several factors affect whether your email is opened, including technical issues such as HTML and spam filters, and non-technical things like time of day, day of week, "from" address and subject line. Of these, the "from" address and subject lines are certainly the easiest to control, and, thus, the easiest to test.

• **"From" address.** The "From" address is the name or address that shows up in your recipient's in-box. You don't have too many options here. I would test your organization name against your executive director's name (if his or her name is well known). By the way, don't use a generic name, like "Volunteer opportunity" or "Online action center." Your recipient won't know which organization you are.

• **Subject lines.** Here are a few possibilities for testing subject lines to increase open rates:

Straightforward vs suggestive subject lines

> Your donation will help a child eat today.
>
> vs.
>
> How can you help the orphans?

To Mention the Ask or Not?

> Looking ahead, more animals need your help
> in the coming year.
>
> vs.
>
> Your gift of $100 will help animals in the coming year.

Subject lines that in different ways ask for a renewal of commitment.

> Renew your commitment for next year.
>
> vs.
>
> Your membership is expiring.
>
> vs.
>
> Renew today – and save even more puppies.

Short or long

> Outrage.
>
> vs.
>
> Outrageous report shows true cost of war.

• **Click through rates.** Efforts to boost your click-through rate (the number of recipients who click on the link to your donation page) give you various testing options. Here are some you might already be familiar with in your direct mail program:

- Premiums. Will offering a CD boost response, at an acceptable cost and hassle factor?

- Offer. Is it specific - "Your gift of $30 will help feed a family of four" or general – "Your gift will feed families"?

- Copy. Short and sweet versus longer and more detailed.

- Link placement. Where do recipients click most frequently? Top right? Or, maybe the P.S.?

• **Conversion rates.** When a person clicks to your donation page, you're half of the way home. Now your job is to blend information, persuasion, and ease in a way that motivates the person to complete the form (if you haven't preprinted their name and address, which is better) and make a gift. Items to experiment with include:

Short vs. long page. Perhaps your prospect has been persuaded by your e-mail to make a gift, and you don't want long copy to stop the momentum. Then again, maybe you'll seal the deal with a sentence or two confirming how your organization will put their contribution to work.

Images and insets. Using a bold, compelling image or quote on the donation page may be just the thing that tips the scales in your direction. Or not.

Giving levels. If you set the lowest dollar level too high, you risk a lower conversion and response rate. But set it too low and you leave money on the table.

While this list isn't exhaustive, testing these common variables is a sound place to start. You'll be pleasantly surprised to learn that even a small change – a slightly reworded subject line, for example, will yield better results.

■ Make sure your test is valid.

Of course, you can't rely on your results, or hope to repeat them, unless you run a valid test. In that vein, keep the following suggestions in mind:

• Decide how you will test. For example, will you send different emails to two small groups, and roll out to the rest of your list when you learn the results? Or will you split your entire e-mail list for the test. Use quantities that generate statistically valid results. If you're testing a variable that will be measured by response rates, you'll need a large sample, say 7,000 to 10,000. To test open rates, a smaller quantity, of around 3,000 to 5,000, will suffice. Consult a significance calculator to guide your decisions.

• Test one variable at a time. Your results will be inconclusive if you do otherwise.

• Be aware that time of day affects your results. Send to your test groups as close together as your e-mail messaging system allows.

• You'll get the majority of your results on the day you send your email (assuming you've sent it early). Still, there will be those who can't check their in-box regularly, so wait at least 24 hours before making any decisions.

I'd like to end this chapter by outing my inner-geek: to me, segmenting and testing is, dare I say it, fun. I've spent many a Friday night playing with results to see just what pearls I could pull out of a report (I do have a life, really).

And it's not only that I'm squeezing out the best results for my clients, though of course that's a motivation too.

I guess what gives me just as much of a thrill – as I shout to my husband that I'll be up shortly – is that what we're learning today is defining our young industry. We're blazing the trail. Setting the standards. Developing the baselines.

I'm a pioneer ... and so are you.

11

Conclusion

What lies ahead for email fundraising?

Will it one day surpass direct mail amd telemarketing, or perhaps be supplanted by another technology we can't conceive of yet?

I can't tell you, nor can anyone else.

But what I can say is this: email and the web are here to stay and this fascinating medium deserves your attention.

In this book I hope I've provided enough guidance to get you started. I further hope I've shown that email fundraising needn't be intimidating – if you take it a step at a time.

In closing, I'd like to summarize each of those key steps for you:

1) Select email messaging and donation processing software that's especially designed for non-profit organizations. And even before then, settle on a smart in-house communication strategy.

2) Build your list! You can't raise money with email if you don't have a list of email addresses. It's a rigorous and unrelenting process.

3) Take advantage of timing. Using email when big news hits is arguably the most important element in raising money with this medium. If you can nail the timing, you'll raise more money online. It's that simple.

4) Use a campaign approach. Don't rely on an isolated email to reach all your constituents. Give your appeal a better chance by sending three, four, or even more emails.

5) Write the right way for the web. Your readers are busy – you have only a few seconds to capture their attention. Make your emails easy to read and easy to scan. And pay special attention to the subject line – it determines whether your email is opened.

6) Bring on the creativity if you can! Cutting through the clutter in your donor's email box isn't easy. Be daring with eye-catching visuals, bold headlines, and irresistible offers. But be yourself, too, and speak from the heart.

7) Integrate your emails with your direct mail and telemarketing program. Offering your donors the convenience of giving through the mail, over the phone, *and* online will pay off.

8) In between your fundraising appeals, cultivate your donors with emails that focus on news, humor, and warmth. It'll be easier to connect with them when you ask for a gift.

9) Learn from the data. Review your results and make decisions on your next move based on how your donors have responded.

10) Segment and test. By identifying what motivates your constituents, and what types of messages they respond to, you'll build a stronger list and generate higher revenue.

And there you have what I believe is a workable 10 step program that will lead to your online success with fundraising.

I began this book by noting three things about email: it's cheap, easy, and everywhere. By now, I'm sure you understand the problems inherent in that. Namely, the potential for expensive mistakes, the ease of bungling your program, and the very real possibility that everything you send will be ignored.

But none of that will happen to you now, will it? You know your way around an in-box. At least you do if I've done my job.

So get going. Chances are your constituents are checking their email right now.

RESOURCES

Throughout this book, I've referred to all kinds of vendors and firms, but I haven't cited any by name. And ... I'm not going to. *But* I will tell you how I'd go about finding vendors if I were you.

First, the kinds of vendors you'll need are:

- Email messaging
- Online donation processing
- Web designers and programmers
- List/name portals and brokers
- Append firms
- Consulting firms

Now, the most obvious and often only solution to finding just the right company is word of mouth. Other users are your best source of information and recommendations.

Beyond word of mouth, I'd do three things:

1) Use the Internet, of course. Head to your favorite search engine and start typing in the terms I list below. You'll begin to see names repeated, and you'll also find there are a number of web sites that aggregate vendors and compare them in one place. Those are very helpful and I'd start there.

When searching for email messaging and online donation processing, note that many vendors offer both of these services in one package and I wouldn't waste time with those that don't.

Search terms that will help you find the people you need are the following:

• Variations on "online fundraising," with "vendor," "software," and "ASP" (application service provider).

• The terms "email marketing" and "email messaging" will overwhelm you with vendors. Add the term "nonprofit" to either of these to narrow down your selection.

• Append vendors can be found by typing in phrases like "append email addresses" with "nonprofit."

• Searching for email list brokers isn't efficient online and you'll find mostly spammers.

• Similarly, it's hard to find the right web designer and programmer by searching online. Don't waste your time.

2) Check out nonprofit and fundraising trade publications. You'll see many of the big names advertising in full-page spreads, and some of the smaller vendors in the classifieds. Since these publications target the nonprofit sector, you'll find many of the right vendors there.

3) Attend professional conferences and association meetings. They usually have workshops on online fundraising featuring recommendations from experienced speakers (hey, like me!).

ACKNOWLEDGMENTS

My dad kept his bills in a shoebox. When it came time to pay them, he always pulled out the "begging letters" first. I remember him saying, "Honey, these are the bills you always pay first." So I guess you have him to blame, and I have him to thank for spending all these years raising money – and writing this book.

It is both fun and humbling to write a book! I highly recommend it – but only if you work with Emerson & Church's Jerry Cianciolo, who made my experience educational and easy (while I made his exasperating and, hmmm, exciting). Thank you, Jerry.

My experience in putting this book together was also eased significantly by the assistance of many other people. I've tried to list them all here.

First, thank you to my colleagues at Donordigital who are such a pleasure to accomplish this work with every day, including those who provided excellent feedback on this book: Farra Trompeter, Jenn Smith, Alia McKee, Rachel Allison, and especially DD founder Nick Allen.

I owe much gratitude to all the Donordigital clients throughout the past six years who have been my partners in learning the lessons in this book, and have offered me the great privilege of working for causes that matter to me.

I am especially grateful to those clients and friends who have allowed me to showcase their work here: America's Second Harvest, ASPCA, Earthjustice, Environmental Defense, Heifer International,

Humane Society of the United States, Human Rights Campaign, Massachusetts SPCA, NARAL Pro-Choice America, the Polly Klaas Foundation, and Union of Concerned Scientists.

Thank you to Mal Warwick who encouraged and championed me in writing this book and so much more.

And, of course, I am eternally grateful to my sweet husband, Scott Connolly, for waiting patiently, reading avidly, complimenting generously, and putting up with the wild schedule that not only allowed me to write this book, but also allows me to pursue the work that I've always dreamed of every day.

ABOUT THE AUTHOR

Madeline Stanionis is the President and Creative Director of Donordigital, a full-service online fundraising, advocacy, and marketing company which helps nonprofit organizations, campaigns, and socially responsible businesses use the Internet to build their constituencies and achieve their goals.

Since 1999, Donordigital has been developing and managing successful programs for major organizations committed to using the Internet to build their constituencies.

Clients include the American Civil Liberties Union, the AARP and the AARP Foundation, Amnesty International USA, the Campaign to Defend the Constitution, Earthjustice, Girl Scouts of the USA, Human Rights Campaign, the Humane Society of the United States, NARAL Pro-Choice America, Parents' Action for Children, Union of Concerned Scientists, and the U.S. Fund for UNICEF. Visit their web site at www.donordigital.com for more information.

Madeline joined Donordigital in 2000, but has been raising money, organizing, and communicating for organizations and causes for 20 years, not counting her second-grade campaign for George McGovern.

She served as director of individual giving at Health Access, a statewide health advocacy organization in California, and as Public Information Officer for the Alameda County Health Department (Berkeley, Oakland). Madeline was the founding executive director of Access to Software for All People (ASAP), a youth-run Web development business run as a non-profit social enterprise.

She is a frequent speaker and writer in fundraising, advocacy, and technology conferences and publications across the country, and co-convenes Web of Change, an international annual gathering that connects global leaders in online communications, technology, and activism who are actively building a better world.

Madeline holds a Masters of Social Work from San Francisco State University. She lives in Berkeley with her husband, Scott Connolly, and two rescued greyhounds, Daisy and Ajax.

The Mercifully Brief, Real World Guide to

RAISING $1,000 GIFTS BY MAIL

by Mal Warwick, 112 pp. $24.95.

Whoever heard of raising $1,000 gifts (not to mention $3,000, $4,000, and $5,000 gifts) by mail? That's the realm of personal solicitation, right?

Not exclusively, says Mal Warwick, in his book, *The Mercifully Brief, Real World Guide to Raising $1,000 Gifts by Mail.*

And Warwick should know. He's spent the last decade and more perfecting the art of *high dollar* direct mail.

Are you skeptical?

Consider just one mailing Warwick cites (and he has more than 100 such mailings to draw from).

A total of 2,352 pieces were mailed to donors who had given $100 or more. This small mailing - now get ready for 'numbers that will blow your socks off,' to use the author's words - this small mailing generated $148,000!

That translates into an *average* gift of $463. But better still, the mailing garnered 54 gifts that topped $1,000. And five of the recipients sent in $5,000 or more.

And what was the final fundraising cost for this effort? About eight cents per dollar raised!

That's the good news (an under-statement, to be sure). The *even better news* is that *you* can generate, if not these stratospheric numbers, at least results that will soar over your current direct mail returns.

How do you do it? Must you tap a hot-shot firm or be a prizewinning writer?

While these wouldn't hurt, of course, Warwick touts self-reliance. He shows you - with carefully selected examples and illustrations along the way - how to succeed on your own, walking you step by step through the process of identifying your prospects, crafting the right letter, the right brochure, the right response device, and the right envelope.

In this remarkable book - about an hour's read - Warwick convinces even the most doubting Thomas. Commit to the strategies he outlines, and you'll be startled, if not astounded, by the results.

From Emerson & Church, Publishers

The Mercifully Brief, Real World Guide to

RAISING MORE MONEY WITH NEWSLETTERS THAN YOU EVER THOUGHT POSSIBLE

by Tom Ahern, 128 pp. $24.95.

Today, countless organizations are raising more money with their newsletter than with traditional mail appeals. And after reading Tom Ahern's riveting book, *Raising More Money with Newsletters than You Ever Thought Possible*, it's easy to understand why.

Great newsletters, as distinguished from the mundane ones many of us receive, have so much more going for them. For starters, they deliver real news (not tired features such as "From the Director's Desk" and "Introducing Our New Staff"). They make the donor feel important. They use emotional triggers to spur action.

They're designed in a way to attract both browsers and readers. And they don't depend on dry statistics to make the organization's case.

Ahern knows newsletters inside and out. So when he speaks - as he does in engaging and eloquent prose - you hang onto his every word.

The essence of *Raising More Money with Newsletters than You Ever Thought Possible* centers around seven fatal flaws, as Ahern calls them. "Almost every donor newsletter I see suffers from at least one of the flaws," he says early in the book. "You would be shocked by how many newsletters suffer from all seven."

Along the way to discussing – and dissecting – these fatal flaws, the reader is treated to such chapters as:

- Making news out of thin air
- What a front page is for
- Lower the grade level of your writing
- Anecdotes versus stats
- How should it look? A proven formula

And those are only five of the *45!* succinct chapters in this book.

Chances are you already have a newsletter, that's the good news. You have the vehicle in place. The even better news is that transforming your newsletter into a substantial money raiser isn't all that difficult.

As Ahern himself says, "You don't need a degree in journalism to publish a newsletter that will keep your donors inspired (and generous). You just need a few skills and insights."

From Emerson & Church, Publishers

The Mercifully Brief, Real World Guide to

ATTRACTING THE ATTENTION YOUR CAUSE DESERVES

by Joseph Barbato, 112 pp. $24.95.

To attract attention to your cause, you could:
- Paint your building Day-Glo orange
- Blare hip hop music from the rooftop
- Have staff members sport Mohawk haircuts

But if you're a bit less bombastic, and searching for innovative (and more palatable) ways to attract *ongoing* attention, you'll fare much better with Joseph Barbato's book, *Attracting the Attention Your Cause Deserves*.

First, let's make clear what this book is NOT. It is *not* a guide for writing press releases. It is *not* a manual for creating a speaker's bureau. It is *not* a treatise offering PR palaver. All of those hairs have been split ... many times over.

Attracting the Attention Your Cause Deserves is something far more useful – and invigorating – to those wanting to advance the good work of their organization. Think of it as a "Trade Secrets Revealed" book, one allowing you to accomplish three key objectives for your cause:

1) Greater visibility
2) A broader constituency
3) More money raised

And who better to write it than Joseph Barbato, a widely respected pro who's worked both sides of the aisle.

After reading *Attracting the Attention Your Cause Deserves*, here are just a few of the skills at which you'll be more proficient:

- Sharpening your organization's niche
- Identifying the range of people who benefit from your work ... thereby targeting your audiences with greater precision
- Cultivating the right media people, locally, regionally, and nationally if appropriate
- Organizing your website most efficiently for the press
- Making a persuasive pitch, in writing and over the phone
- Becoming the "go to" person for reporters and others, and
- Learning how to package your expertise to gain even greater exposure

Take Barbato's insider wisdom to heart. It spills over every single page of this book. Then, even if you whisper, you'll still be heard.

From Emerson & Church, Publishers

OPEN IMMEDIATELY!
STRAIGHT TALK ON DIRECT MAIL FUNDRAISING:
WHAT WORKS, WHAT DOESN'T, AND WHY

by Stephen Hitchcock, 259 pp., $24.95.

If you want straight talk about direct mail fundraising, do what the title says: open this book immediately.

In it you'll find 81 chapters examining virtually every topic of importance to those who raise money by mail.

Unlike other books that over-complicate the subject, *Open Immediately!*, by Stephen Hitchcock, does just the opposite. It offers an elegantly simple and inviting approach to direct mail by focusing on one element at a time. (This approach has the added benefit of making it easy to find the exact help you need.)

The book is divided into six major parts:
• Essentials of Direct Mail Fundraising
• Acquiring and Renewing Donors
• Targeting Your Mailings
• Writing Effective Letters
• Key Components of Your Appeal, and
• How to Ask

Within each part, Hitchcock offers specific suggestions with just enough detail to allow you to implement his advice. Take the section, 'How to Ask.' Among the topics discussed are: ways of asking for the gift, why it's important to ask for the gift at least twice, when *not* to ask for a specific gift, how to increase the *first* gift (the key one as it dictates the size of future gifts), how to raise $1,000 gifts by mail, and how to ask for monthly gifts and charitable bequests. And that's just a sampling.

Or take the section, 'Key Components of Your Appeal.' The 16 topics Hitchcock explores in these pages include a discussion of obsolete (and offensive) techniques, the cardinal rules of envelope copy, the misunderstood role of inserts, the use of multiple signatures, how to contain your costs, even a look at URGENT telegrams and whether they work.

With its clear-eyed realistic focus, there's no other book on direct mail fundraising quite like *Open Immediately!* Hitchcock knows that your time is limited. He realizes too that you're not going to upend your current program. But what you can do, he understands, is tweak your efforts to be more profitable. And, *Open Immediately!* offers you dozens and dozens of ways to do just this.

From Emerson & Church, Publishers

INDEX

Copies of this book are available
from the publisher at discount
when purchased in quantity.

Emerson
& Church
PUBLISHERS

P.O. Box 338 • Medfield, MA 02052
Tel. 508-359-0019 • Fax 508-359-2703
www.emersonandchurch.com